The TRAGEDY of COMPROMISE
The Origin and Impact of the New Evangelicalism

Ernest D. Pickering

 Bob Jones University Press
Greenville, South Carolina 29614

Library of Congress Cataloging-in-Publication Data

Pickering, Ernest D.
    The tragedy of compromise : the origin and impact of the new
Evangelicalism / Ernest D. Pickering.
       p.   cm.
    Includes bibliographical references and index.
    ISBN 0-89084-757-6
      1. Evangelicalism—United States—History—20th century.
    2. Evangelicalism—Controversial literature.   3. Fundamentalism.
    I. Title.
    BR1642.U5P49   1994
    277.3′0825—dc20   94-11036
                                            CIP

The Tragedy of Compromise:
The Origin and Impact of the New Evangelicalism
by Ernest D. Pickering

Cover designed by Doug Young
Edited by Mark Sidwell

© 1994 Bob Jones University Press
Greenville, South Carolina 29614

Printed in the United States of America

ISBN 0-89084-757-6

15 14 13 12 11 10 9 8 7 6 5 4 3 2 1

$\mathcal{D}\,\mathcal{H}$

Table of Contents

Foreword

There he goes again!

Dr. Ernest Pickering, the diligent scholar, excellent teacher, and practical preacher who has excited Christians in many places, and especially in Russia, by writing *Biblical Separation,* has written another book, *The Tragedy of Compromise.*

In this book he traces the idea of compromise in various stages. He shows how ecclesiastics have used the various forms of compromise to produce the philosophy into which neo-evangelicalism has developed. The book is thorough. Dr. Pickering has keen insight into the various theological teachings and sheds the light of reason and revelation on the many views he discusses.

This book is a "must" for pastors, students, and local church leaders and teachers.

Monroe Parker, Ph.D., D.D., L.L.D.
General Director
Baptist World Mission

Introduction

It has been said that politics is "the fine art of compromise." This may be true of pragmatic politics, but it certainly ought not to be true of Christian theology. Years ago a history of the National Association of Evangelicals bore the title, *Cooperation Without Compromise.* Although few would dispute the accuracy of the first word in describing the NAE, many would raise serious questions about the last two.

There are times when compromise may be wise and good. In the everyday interaction of life, there are times when individuals or groups must come from more extreme positions to a middle ground. Husbands and wives must sometimes yield to one another. Committees striving to solve problems and establish goals must agree to common terms. Persons of goodwill learn to surrender personal preferences to achieve a mutually agreeable solution. This kind of compromise is right and good and promotes a more harmonious relationship between human beings. In other words, not all compromise is evil.

On the other hand, there are certain truths, convictions, and positions which cannot be compromised. Martin Luther, pressed by his political and ecclesiastical foes, rightly refused to renounce his writings and said to his opponents, "Here I stand; I can do no other." Athanasius, champion of the complete deity of Christ against the Arians who denied it, was warned by a colleague, "The whole world is against you." Replied Athanasius, "Then I am against the whole world." There would be no compromise for him on a matter so crucial.

Compromise on matters vital to the Christian faith can very gradually lead an individual, church, or institution away from the sound teaching of the Word of God. The New Evangelicalism has been a siren voice to draw people away from a straight biblical course toward the rocks of spiritual disaster.

W. B. Riley, famous fundamentalist leader and long-time pastor of the First Baptist Church of Minneapolis, in speaking of the

Jebusites, Hivites, Amalekites, and assorted other "ites" warned that the most dangerous of all were the "in-betweenites." These are the folks who try to straddle every issue and keep friends on both sides. Dr. Bob Jones, Sr., likened them to a man who, during the Civil War, decided to try to save his neck by wearing a Confederate jacket and Union pants. The Yankees fired at his jacket and the Rebels at his pants. He could not win for losing. It does not pay to compromise.

In this study, while not hesitating to name names, we seek primarily to deal with principles. Names change, and leaders come and go, but principles remain the same.

Obviously, in addressing such issues as are before us, there will be disagreements among fundamentalists on some points of interpretation. However, in spite of such disagreements, true fundamentalists should be united in their stand against the unscriptural teachings of New Evangelicalism.

Some may wonder at the propriety of publicly challenging the convictions and practices of fellow believers. There is good precedent, however. When the great leader of the early church, Peter, defected in doctrine and practice, the Apostle Paul said, "I withstood him to the face, because he was to be blamed" (Gal. 2:11). There is a proper time for confronting believers who are straying from the truth. The time is now.

I am deeply indebted to my wife, Yvonne, for her long hours of work in editing, revising, and reproducing the final manuscript for this book. Her continual encouragement is a great help to me. Appreciation is also given to Mrs. Dennis Whitehead, my former secretary, for typing the first draft. My son, Lloyd, the "computer whiz" of the family, helped immensely in technical areas. Many thanks also to the skilled staff at Bob Jones University Press for their excellent work in the final publication of this book.

Wolves in Sheep's Clothing

The Fundamentalist-Modernist Controversy

It was our Lord Himself who warned, "Beware of false prophets, which come to you in sheep's clothing, but inwardly they are
ravening wolves" (Matt 7:15). Paul likewise warned of those
"ravening wolves" who would rise up from within the flock to prey
upon the helpless sheep (Acts 20:29). The point in both passages is
that wolves can look like sheep. Thus is the deceptive nature of
Satan's ploys. His agents have "crept in" (a phrase in Jude 4
indicating subtlety and stealthiness). It should come as no surprise
that the satanic method would be to infiltrate the church, the body
of Christ. By so doing his evil majesty could impede tremendously
the progress of the gospel.

The Poison from Europe

The seventeenth and eighteenth centuries saw the rise of new
systems of thought which undermined biblical Christianity. This
era of human history has become known as the Enlightenment.
However, rather than giving light to mankind, it merely com-
pounded the darkness by rejecting divine revelation, which is the
only source of true enlightenment.

Spawned in the minds of unregenerate scholars in England and
on the continent of Europe, deism, naturalism, and rationalism
began to eat like a cancer at the vitals of the Christian faith. Here
were originated the systems of thought that eventually undergirded
the movement called modernism, over which a tremendous theological battle raged in the twentieth century. Men such as John
Locke, the Earl of Shaftesbury, Voltaire, Jean Jacques Rousseau,
Christian Wolff, and Immanuel Kant laid the foundations for the
great apostasy which later overwhelmed the professing church.

To these men the Enlightenment was an emergence of mankind
from a period of immaturity marked by a dependence upon external

authorities such as the Bible and the church. No more would mortals need to be bound by the rigors of fixed dogmas. Now men could engage in "free thought," unfettered by outdated theological concepts. The "miraculous" must be judged in the light of human reason, they said. No longer could one be credulous and accept biblical accounts as authentic. One must think for himself apart from that which claimed to be divine revelation. No more should men view the Bible as authoritative. Scholarly pens were echoing the utterance of the prince of liars, "Yea, hath God said . . . ?" (Gen 3:1).

On the wave of the Enlightenment came an infatuation with the theory of evolution. It was a convenient way in which to explain the existence of the universe without the embarrassment of having to introduce a divine being. It fitted in perfectly with the humanistic framework of thought that was developing. Religion to these "enlightened" ones was a continually developing human effort to find answers to life's questions, rather than a humble response to divine revelation. Man was evolving in his understanding of God. He was moving out of the darkness of credulity into a fuller understanding of his potential. For this reason, the "enlightened" welcomed the postulate of a scholar such as Rousseau that men are essentially good.

The Enlightenment had a profound impact upon the Christian church. While some of its doctrines were later attacked by other thinkers, many of the fundamental concepts introduced by the writers in this Age of Reason became a part of that system called modernism that spread like a plague throughout Christendom.

German philosophers such as Georg Hegel were among the fathers of the liberalism of the nineteenth century. He set out to reconcile theology and philosophy as well as religion and reason. His concept of the dialectical nature of thought had a profound impact upon later theologians. There is no permanency of truth, according to Hegel; even God is changing. Hegel's approach paved the way for the complete removal of religious thought from the realm of the absolute to the realm of the tentative and subjective. He emphasized the intellectual element in religious thought to the detriment of biblical exegesis.

A fellow German who had a tremendous impact upon religious thought was Friedrich Schleiermacher. His emphasis was on religious experience. True religion for him was a feeling of dependency upon the "Infinite" (not, in his thinking, a personal God). A Christian believer is one who has had an "experience," an intuition of his own. Thus, Christianity is not grounded in objective, complete, and final divine revelation, but in the "felt experiences" of its adherents. This patently false teaching has permeated the modern church and has devastated it.

Theological Liberalism

Out of the matrix of this European mix of unbelief came the movement known in church history as modernism, now often referred to as theological liberalism. What are some hallmarks of liberalism?

1. A rejection of the historic Christian doctrine of biblical inspiration.
2. A tolerance of all views that come from within the religious community.
3. An emphasis upon the validity of human experience over the revealed truth of God.
4. A denial of the absolute and unique deity of Christ.
5. An emphasis on the dignity and goodness of man.
6. A rejection of the total depravity of man and the resultant necessity of the new birth.
7. An evolutionary concept of the origin of all things as opposed to a creationist view.
8. A rejection of the supernatural interventions of God in human history.
9. An emphasis upon the social gospel, that is, that the main mission of the church is to correct societal ills. Sin is essentially social and thus salvation must involve the correction of these social problems.

Armed with this theology, liberal leaders within the established denominations began to exercise considerable influence. Liberalism became the dominant view at most denominational theological seminaries. During the latter part of the nineteenth century, the growing power of liberal thought began to be apparent. The liberals argue that vast changes have occurred in the world since the time of Christ and that Christianity, to be successful, must change also. We must affirm, they claim, the "abiding experiences" of the faith within a theological and cultural context that is acceptable to modern man. Since they controlled the ecclesiastical apparatus in most of the denominations, they were able to spread their doctrines profusely. The words of Scripture came to pass: "Now the Spirit speaketh expressly, that in the latter times some shall depart from the faith, giving heed to seducing spirits, and doctrines of devils" (I Tim 4:1).[1]

Liberalism Challenged

The Almighty God did not let the attack upon His Word go unchallenged. Multitudes of valiant warriors of the cross arose to do battle with the hosts of darkness. Interdenominational Bible conferences began to emerge in various locations. Here the great truths of the historic Christian faith were expounded by such men as James Brookes, W. E. Blackstone, A. T. Pierson, C. I. Scofield, A. C. Gaebelein, James M. Gray, and many others. The Niagara Bible Conference was among the earliest of these and was joined by numerous others including those at Winona Lake, Indiana, and Montrose, Pennsylvania. Great crowds gathered for many years at such sites and heard stirring biblical messages reaffirming the teachings of God's Word.

About 1910, Lyman Stewart, one of the founders of what became the Union Oil Company and a dedicated Christian, decided to fund the publication of some booklets to which were given the general title *The Fundamentals*. Great Christian scholars and preachers contributed articles on such doctrines as the virgin birth of Christ, the inspiration of Scripture, the bodily resurrection of the Lord, the atonement, and other vital issues. Those espousing these historic Christian doctrines became known popularly as fundamentalists.

Some fundamentalist leaders, sensing the need for a more concerted stand against the strong liberalism of the day decided to found a new organization. Thus in 1919 they organized in Philadelphia the World's Christian Fundamentals Association. W. B. Riley, pastor of the First Baptist Church of Minneapolis, Minnesota, was its first president. The organization was an important milestone in the development of the fundamentalist movement.

Tremendous controversies took place as fundamentalists struggled to expose and oppose the Bible-denying modernists who were sapping the very life from the churches of Christ. A monumental conflict took place within the Presbyterian Church in the U.S.A., centering on that historic educational institution—Princeton Seminary. J. Gresham Machen, an outstanding New Testament scholar, led a protest against the rising liberalism within the Presbyterian denomination and within Princeton Seminary itself. As a result of the conflict, the Bible-defending professors left to form another seminary, and Princeton swiftly fell to the forces of liberalism.

Baptists were not spared from the theological and ecclesiastical turmoil. Repeatedly fundamentalist leaders within the Northern Baptist Convention sought to position the denomination on a biblical base, but their efforts were continually thwarted by the political machinations of the liberals. Frustrated by these repeated defeats, fundamentalists began to take other measures. The Conservative Baptist Foreign Mission Society was formed and later the Conservative Baptist Home Mission Society, both of which purposed to receive missionary funds from churches within the Northern Baptist Convention that were unhappy with the liberal program. The Conservative Baptist Association began, and it gradually became separated from the convention. Many churches pulled out of the convention completely and affiliated with the General Association of Regular Baptist Churches.

Other great champions of the faith arose within various communions. William McCarrell led some churches out of Congregationalism and founded the Independent Fundamental Churches of America. Robert ("Fighting Bob") Shuler, long-time pastor of the great Trinity Methodist Church in Los Angeles, fought the liberals in his denomination through the pages of his paper, *The Methodist Challenge*. Voices such as that of J. Frank Norris challenged the apostasy that was growing within the Southern Baptist Convention. It was not easy to take such a bold stand for the faith. It cost many of these men lifelong friendships. They were held up to ridicule in the public press as well as in denominational periodicals, and their character was vilified. They were viewed as "troublers of Israel," but they persisted in their defense of those doctrines which they held precious. At the conclusion of their ministries, when they reported in heaven to the Lord of the church, they could say with the great apostle, "I have fought a good fight, I have finished my course, I have kept the faith" (II Tim 4:7).

Granted, these men had "warts" and "feet of clay." In more recent years some critics have specialized in uncovering all the "dirt" that might be attached to some fundamentalist leaders. Certainly they had faults, but they stood courageously for the eternal truths of the Word of God in the time of trouble. For this they must be honored.

Sadly, it must be noted, some grow weary of the battle and wish to "lay their armor down." Fundamentalists must take heed to the warnings by one worthy chronicler of the movement: "Virtually all spiritual movements have ultimately diminished in vigor and strength of conviction. Truths once held dynamically came to be held only formally. . . . New leadership emerges that paid no price of suffering. To them the battles have ended. . . . The only true Fundamentalist is a fighting Fundamentalist."[2]

Notes

[1]For beliefs and background of liberalism note the following works. For philosophic and historical development, see J. L. Neve, *A History of Christian Thought,* vol. 2, book five, chaps. 1-7. For a defense of liberalism, see Donald Miller, *The Case for Liberal Christianity.* For a refutation of liberalism, see J. Grescham Machen, *Christianity and Liberalism.*

[2]David Beale, *In Pursuit of Purity,* pp. 356-57.

Developing the Art of Fence-Straddling

Beginnings and Growth of the New Evangelicalism

In the 1920s and 1930s, the lines of battle were clearly drawn between fundamentalism and modernism. Tremendous controversies had erupted within the various denominations. The struggles were hard and often bitter. The future of churches, colleges, seminaries, and mission boards was at stake. Bible-believing people had poured their lives and their resources into these entities and were loathe to let them fall into the hands of the enemies of the truth.

Yet as the battle went on, some became weary of it. Not all were content to be "fighting fundamentalists," and the controversy had continued far too long to suit some. It was time, thought they, for a change of approach. Out of this attitude of mind sprang that movement we refer to as the "New Evangelicalism."

New Winds Blowing

Years ago a noted fundamentalist accurately declared that the New Evangelicalism was born with a "mood." It is difficult to define a "mood," but it is nonetheless very real and potent. A person in a foul mood can cause problems aplenty. Conversely, one who is in a good mood can uplift the spirits of all around him. Unfortunately, the mood that was developing among certain young fundamentalists was one of restiveness and dissatisfaction with the ongoing conflict with the liberals.

No doubt this mood was spawned in part by the embarrassing antics of some fundamentalists and the pugnacious and unkind spirit of others. Some fundamentalist leaders were cantankerous and very hard to get along with. Unnecessary "turf fights" arose, and some fundamentalists made vicious personal attacks on others. This spirit on the part of some disheartened younger men, and coupled with other factors that will be discussed later, propelled them toward a softer and broader position.

Honest fundamentalists must admit that some of their number have been guilty of excesses and unscriptural behavior. Some have walked in the flesh and not the Spirit. Some have insisted that everyone with whom they fellowship must cross every *t* and dot every *i* in the same way that they do. In other words, fundamentalists have demonstrated amply the fact that they also have "old natures." This fact, however, does not justify embracing an erroneous philosophy, theology, or methodology. The author through the years has reminded younger preachers that they ought not to reject a scriptural position because some fundamentalists have proven to be an embarrassment to the cause.

A Developing Compromise Position

Harold Ockenga, long-time pastor of Park Street Church in Boston, claimed to have originated the term "New Evangelical" in a convocation speech at Fuller Theological Seminary made in 1948. Ockenga, who also was the first president of Fuller Theological Seminary, is often called "the father of the New Evangelicalism." As a respected pastor and noted scholar, Ockenga had tremendous influence.

What factors spurred the rise of this position called the "New Evangelicalism"? No doubt several could be cited, but the following six are certainly significant.

1. A reaction to what was perceived as excessive negativism on the part of fundamentalists

Early New Evangelical leaders took great pains to emphasize the fact that fundamentalists were too much "against" and not enough "for." Their plea was "Let's be positive and not negative." While this statement has an emotional appeal to many, it is not a biblical philosophy. Scripture is both positive and negative—it is *for* some things and *against* others. We must strive for that same balance.

2. A desire to be accepted by the scholarly world

Many young fundamentalist scholars became resentful of the fact that they were not viewed with respect by fellow scholars in their special disciplines. Because they were fundamentalists, they were viewed as deficient intellectually, and their work was not recognized by the scholarly world as a whole. This grated upon them and motivated them to adjust their views and their style so as to become more acceptable to the intellectual leaders of the day. There were Christians in the apostolic churches who had a similar bent, causing Paul to say, "Beware lest any man spoil you through philosophy and vain deceit, after the tradition of men, after the rudiments of the world, and not after Christ" (Col. 2:8). The desire to be intellectually respectable in the eyes of a godless world has ruined many a promising scholar.

3. The influence of training in liberal institutions

A man generally reflects the philosophy of the schools where he was trained. Many young fundamentalist scholars in the 1940s, 1950s, and 1960s enrolled in liberal institutions in this country and abroad in order to pursue graduate education. While they did not always imbibe everything they were taught, they were greatly influenced in many of their positions by the unbelievers under whom they studied. To them, it was a "broadening" experience. But one is reminded of the wry observation of Vance Havner years ago when he said, "What some people feel is their mind broadening is only their conscience stretching." While some men have been able to weather the storms of unbelief while studying at liberal institutions, many are unable to do so and come out tainted with unbiblical notions.

4. The general mindset and spirit of the age

Dogmatism was becoming a hated concept. There was a call for "openness" and the acceptance of varying viewpoints as at least viable options for the believer. New hermeneutical approaches were becoming fashionable among so-called evangelicals, who hailed the irenic spirit in place of the militant spirit. This irenic spirit was part of the warp and woof of the New Evangelicalism.

5. A reaction to the criticism that fundamentalism lacked a vision for social action

The early 1900s had seen a tremendous increase in enthusiasm for social programs to correct perceived ills in society and to equalize the status of citizens. This produced the so-called social gospel which captured the mainline denominations and replaced the preaching and teaching of the Word of God. While

New Evangelicals did not go as far as did liberals in embracing this new emphasis, they were definitely influenced by it. Stung by continuing criticisms that fundamentalists were lacking in concern for the poor and needy, New Evangelicals sought to introduce a wider "social consciousness." Carl Henry's book *The Uneasy Conscience of Modern Fundamentalism* sounded this note.

6. A growing ecumenical spirit which viewed fundamentalists as too separatistic

The ecumenical movement was gaining momentum in the 1950s and 1960s at the same time the New Evangelicalism was arising. "Let's get together"—this was the cry. Evangelicals were influenced by this aim as well. "Perhaps we have been too narrow. Let us open our arms of fellowship to others with whom we may not fully agree." Forgotten (or repudiated) was the injunction of the Apostle John: "If there come any unto you, and bring not this doctrine, receive him not into your house, neither bid him God speed: for he that biddeth him God speed is partaker of his evil deeds" (II John 10-11).

As a result of these factors, and perhaps others, a movement known as the New Evangelicalism began to grow apace. The term *fundamentalist* was rejected in favor of the term *evangelical.* In an early issue of *Christianity Today* the editor remarked, "A growing preference for the term *evangelicalism* has developed within recent years. . . . The alternate, *fundamentalism,* has narrower content and has acquired unbiblical accretions."[1] While they were definitely changing, they did not want the fundamentalist public to know that they were changing too much. They had a "hidden agenda," as it were. Their struggles to be New Evangelicals while still appearing to be fundamentalists are recounted in some detail in Marsden's fascinating book, *Reforming Fundamentalism.* The liberal organ *Christian Century,* in evaluating the rising New Evangelicalism, astutely observed that it was led by "a group of younger men who are impatient with fundamentalism as they find it. They call themselves the new evangelicals. . . . They must wear the old garments of fundamentalism while changing the man within."[2] Another expressed it this way: "The new evangelicals . . . are actually trying to rehabilitate the old fundamentalism. . . . The new evangelicalism is really the old fundamentalism."[3]

Although there is a historic connection between fundamentalism and New Evangelicalism, the contrasts began to appear at an early stage. There were differences in emphasis, in spirit, and in perceptions of the church and its purpose. Marsden described the New Evangelical approach in this way:

> They [the New Evangelicals] continued to oppose liberalism in theology, but dropped militancy as a primary aspect of their identity. They were willing to reevaluate some of their own theological heritage, often dropping dispensationalism though not usually premillennialism, and allowing debate at least on the question of the inerrancy of Scripture. Aspiring to be a broad coalition of theologically conservative Protestants, they usually tolerated some other doctrinal differences, including Pentecostalism. Evangelism, as epitomized by Billy Graham, remained their central activity, although the forms of presentation now sometimes avoided accentuation of the offensiveness of the gospel.[4]

Milestones Along the Road to Compromise

New Evangelicals desired a more united voice and some organizational structure through which their principles could be promulgated. This desire resulted in the founding of the National Association of Evangelicals in 1942. At nearly the same time, Carl McIntire organized the American Council of Christian Churches. The two organizations held discussions, but the leaders of the incipient NAE viewed the ACCC as too militant, too separatistic, and too vocal against the ecumenical movement and its leaders. They felt that this approach would hinder them from accomplishing their goals. The NAE has become a leading organizational vehicle for the spread of New Evangelicalism.

The founding of Fuller Theological Seminary in Pasadena, California, in 1947, was another milestone, and a monumental one indeed. One writer has described it as "the leading center of learning for the evangelical left."[5] In a circular letter from the president to the school's constituency, Edward J. Carnell noted, "Our stated purpose is to produce a *great evangelism* by combining *great learning* with *great love* . . . to produce a 'new evangelicalism.' "[6] The name of the school was taken from its benefactor and founder, Charles Fuller, director of the famous radio broadcast "The Old Fashioned Revival Hour," but its theological position soon bore little resemblance to that for which Fuller had become known.

In March of 1956 the fundamentalist world was shaken by an article in a then-popular magazine *Christian Life* entitled, "Is Evangelical Theology Changing?" Some key contributors to that article were Terrelle Crum, Dean, Providence-Barrington Bible College; Vernon Grounds, President, Conservative Baptist Theological Seminary; Carl F. H. Henry, Professor of Systematic Theology, Fuller Seminary; Lloyd Kalland, Professor of Religion, Gordon Theological Seminary; Kenneth Kantzer, Professor of Bible, Wheaton College; and Warren Young, Dean, Northern Baptist Theological Seminary. The article confirmed that which many already knew—leading persons, formerly called "fundamentalists," were moving away from the original position of fundamentalism toward a broader and more accommodating stance.

Also in the year 1956, *Christianity Today* began publication. It was created in some sense to counter the influence of the leading voice of theological liberalism—*Christian Century*. Encouraged by Billy Graham and promoted by other New Evangelical leaders, it quickly became a widely known and respected voice for the new movement.

In 1957 the tide began to turn with regard to large evangelistic crusades. Billy Graham, a rising star on the evangelistic horizon, decided to broaden his approach and conducted his first ecumenical crusade in New York City. Many of his friends warned against it, and many refused to cooperate, but he persisted in his course. The liberal churches of the great metropolis were mobilized in the crusade, and Graham's course was set for the remainder of his ministry.

In the late 1950s and the early 1960s a tremendous battle ensued within the Conservative Baptist movement over the New Evangelicalism. The Conservative Baptist Seminary in Denver, Colorado, under the leadership of Vernon Grounds, became the center of New Evangelical teaching. This teaching was opposed by Pillsbury College, led by Monroe Parker; San Francisco Conservative Baptist Theological Seminary, led by Arno and Archer Weniger; and Central Conservative Baptist Theological Seminary, founded by Richard V. Clearwaters. Hundreds of churches were lost to the Conservative Baptist Movement, and a new mission board was born—the World Conservative Baptist Mission (now called Baptist World Mission). Many of the departing churches remained unaffiliated. Some became part of the New Testament Association of Baptist Churches. This battle was but one example of the conflicts that the New Evangelicalism created.

The Principles of the New Evangelicalism

How did the founders of the New Evangelicalism view themselves? What were the principles they were seeking to establish? One of the more penetrating evaluations of the developing New Evangelicalism was found in the pages of the liberal *Christian Century.* The writer noted with some bemused interest the early beginnings of the movement. He especially pinpointed the difference in mood between the fundamentalists and the New Evangelicals.

A new generation of earnest intellectuals is appearing within the ranks of avowedly fundamentalist groups and educational institutions. These thinkers do not personally bear the battle scars which marked the leaders who engaged in the earlier and futile fight to halt "modernism," and they are not themselves at present embroiled in major struggles of ecclesiastical politics. A strand of irenicism runs through their thought. They are able to view other kinds of theology more objectively and appreciatively than their predecessors did. . . . A new flexibility is developing in their restatement of Protestant orthodoxy and with it a capacity to make their case in terms more sensitive to the integrity of the modern mind.[7]

Harold Ockenga summarized the goals of the New Evangelicalism as follows:

1. They were concerned about the contemporary culture that has lost touch with the true God and desired to see a revival of the Christian faith that would have a significant impact upon secular culture.
2. They lamented the lack of respect for evangelicalism in academic circles and desired to see a measure of respectability regained through the efforts of capable scholars who could defend Christianity on intellectual grounds.
3. They wanted to recapture the leadership of the denominations from the liberals.
4. They desired to see the church be an instrument in producing societal reforms.[8]

Point number three should be specially noted. The process of "infiltration" (the effort to gradually wrest control of the denominations from the liberals) has no support in the Word of God. The instruction there is plain. Are there those who have a "form of godliness" (an outward profession of the Christian faith) but who are "denying the power thereof"? If so, what are we to do? "From such turn away" (II Tim. 3:5). The tragic failure of New Evangelicalism is seen on every hand today. The denominations in which many of them have remained are no more orthodox than they were those years ago. "Evil men and seducers shall wax worse and worse, deceiving, and being deceived" (II Tim. 3:13). We will not turn the tide of unbelief; it will roll on to a great culmination in the monstrous Harlot of the future (Rev. 17).

Another, more detailed outline of New Evangelical principles was given in *Christian Life* in March 1956. The article enumerated eight points concerning the rising movement:

1. "a friendly attitude toward secular science"
2. "a willingness to re-examine beliefs concerning the work of the Holy Spirit"
3. "a more tolerant attitude toward varying views on eschatology"
4. "a shift away from so-called extreme dispensationalism"
5. "an increased emphasis on scholarship"
6. "a more definite recognition of social responsibility"
7. "a re-opening of the subject of biblical inspiration"
8. "a growing willingness of evangelical theologians to converse with liberal theologians."

Since these represent the earliest summary of the principles of the New Evangelicalism, a few comments are in order.

The Problem of Science

Attempts were being made to reconcile the teachings of the Bible with the various scientific theories that were current. New Evangelical scholars seemed embarrassed to observe that the world view of fundamentalists was so extremely contrary to the world view of liberals. Therefore, they felt obliged to try to span the gap. Carl Henry, one of the original architects of the New Evangelicalism, in later years lamented the fact that younger men had gone too far in seeking to mollify pagans.

"Cognitive bargaining" among evangelicals came with a younger generation of scholars, among them Edward John Carnell at Fuller

Seminary . . . and Arthur Holmes at Wheaton College. . . . [A book by Holmes], in presenting theistic evolution, ignores serious criticisms of Darwinian evolution coming even from contemporary scientists. Wheaton modified its earlier statement on divine creation to accommodate theistic evolution, although insisting that human origin be related to miraculous divine intervention.[9]

The efforts to reconcile biblical teaching on the physical universe to demonic substitutions were not motivated primarily by biblical exegesis but by a desire to make the Christian view more acceptable to godless intellectuals. Paul warns us not to seek to "make a fair show in the flesh" (Gal. 6:12). The phrase means "to make a good show outwardly," to seek to impress men and thus remove the offense of the cross.

The Work of the Spirit

The "willingness to re-examine beliefs concerning the work of the Holy Spirit" opened up the way for the flood tide of charismatic teaching with which the church has been inundated in recent years. The formation of such groups as the NAE gave Pentecostalism and the new charismatic movement a "place in the sun" that they had not enjoyed previously. Even though many New Evangelical scholars did not espouse these views, the fact that they would tolerate them without rebuke gave such views a springboard within the evangelical community.

Prophetic Interpretations

The toleration of various eschatological views is also mentioned as a hallmark of the New Evangelical position. Until the 1950s the majority of fundamentalists had been premillennialists, and a large number dispensationalists (although there were fundamentalists who were neither, such as T. T. Shields). Now more openness was hailed as a sign of growing maturity. Years ago this writer was invited to lecture at a New Evangelical seminary on the subject "Why I Am a Fundamentalist." Following the lecture and a question-and-answer session, I was invited to coffee with the faculty. While chitchatting in the faculty lounge, I asked the professor of theology what scheme of eschatology was espoused by the seminary and taught in the classroom. He laughed and replied, "I teach them all. And when we get to the end of the course, the students don't even know what I believe." He viewed this as masterful

15

instruction. One, however, is reminded of the pedagogy of our Lord, of whom it was said, "He taught them as one having authority, and not as the scribes" (Matt. 7:29). In answering biblical questions the scribes were wont to use circuitous reasoning, quoting many scholars, and avoiding dogmatism on disputed points. Christ, on the other hand, spoke plainly and with authority.

Dispensationalism

As already mentioned, a large number of the early fundamentalists were dispensationalists. (Not all fundamentalists were, or are, dispensationalists, however.) The system of teaching known as dispensationalism had been popularized through the Scofield Bible and also through the training provided by a large number of Bible colleges and seminaries. The New Evangelicals disliked dispensationalism. One of the primary causes of their dislike was what they called a "pessimistic" view of world history and particularly of ecclesiastical history. The dispensationalist accepted the teaching that there would be a growing apostasy in the church for which there was no remedy but separation. New Evangelicals were not separatists and hence resisted the inevitable conclusions brought about by the acceptance of dispensationalist thought. New Evangelicals opposed what they saw as the dispensationalist view of the church—"a refuge in a ruined culture."[10] They tended to adopt rather the "Calvinistic-Puritan view that the church must play a central civilization-building role."[11] In discussing the battle of early fundamentalists against liberalism, Marsden notes that many of them began to reject the notion that the apostates could be driven out and were increasingly embracing the conviction that obedient Christians must separate from apostasy. "Dispensational premillennial interpretations of history, which had spread widely among fundamentalists, supported this separatist tendency. . . . By the 1930s the strictest fundamentalists increasingly were proclaiming the duty of ecclesiastical separation."[12] Further in his discussion he adds: "Dispensationalism's pessimistic view of the prevailing culture encourages de-emphasis on social causes in the movement. Dispensationalism's negative estimate of major churches encouraged separatism."[13]

Scholarship

Budding New Evangelicals became restive because their contributions were being virtually ignored by the scholarly world. We should not wonder, however, that fundamentalist scholars, loyal to the inerrancy of Scripture and intellectually submitted to the authority of God's Word, would find little enthusiasm for their work among the purveyors of error. The Word of God through Jeremiah (certainly a "scholarly" work because it was produced by the Holy Spirit) was nevertheless cut to ribbons in scorn by the king's penknife (Jer. 36:23-24). Biblical truth is ever "foolishness" to the unbeliever and more especially to the educated unbeliever (I Cor. 1:18). Paul did not attempt to proclaim God's Word in the "enticing words of man's wisdom" (I Cor. 2:4) but rather in the power of the Holy Spirit.

New Evangelicals tended to view fundamentalists as obscurantists and as anti-intellectuals. This opinion no doubt sprang from the fact that fundamentalists were suspicious of the great citadels and leaders of learning who were almost altogether radical opponents of biblical truth. The intellectual world is, by and large, a world controlled by the master of evil, Satan himself. Fundamentalists accepted the plain teaching of Scripture concerning them: "Having the understanding darkened, being alienated from the life of God through the ignorance that is in them, because of the blindness of their heart" (Eph. 4:18). Many of those seeking intellectual respectability for the faith down through the centuries have often become the church's worst enemies.

> The role of intellectuals in undermining established ideologies (albeit, even unintentionally) at least since the Enlightenment is well documented. . . . The irony in the Evangelical case is that the emphasis placed upon gaining intellectual credibility for the Evangelical position (from the later 1940s to the present) may ultimately have the unintended consequence of undermining the Evangelical position. What began as an enterprise to defend orthodoxy openly and with intellectual integrity, may result in the weakening or even the demise of orthodoxy as it has been defined for the better part of this century. To come full circle, the weakening of the plausibility of traditionalist approaches to the Bible among Evangelical intellectuals appears to be foreshadowing a similar dynamic among the larger Evangelical population. The pattern is well documented. Philosophical innovations, and ideas generally originating from an elitist echelon in society have a marked proclivity for filtering down to the rest of society's population.[14]

17

In honesty we must admit, however, that some fundamentalists do evidence an anti-intellectual attitude. Such persons shy away from or are critical of earnest attempts by even godly fundamentalists to explore the full riches of Scripture. These fundamentalists content themselves with a "surface" approach.

There is a proper balance to be sought. Our minds must be completely submitted to God and the authority of His revelation. We must be "bringing into captivity every thought to the obedience of Christ" (II Cor. 10:5). God has given our minds to be used for His glory. "Gird up the loins of your mind" (I Pet. 1:13) is the divine command. This passage certainly tells us plainly that our minds are important and that the Christian faith does have an intellectual expression.

Social Involvement

Carl Henry was one of the chief purveyors of the concept that the church of Christ should be more heavily involved in social action. In defending this concept Henry wrote,

> From social and political withdrawal to cobelligerency with conservative Catholics and other Americans is a long stride, but some evangelical spokesmen are eagerly encouraging this promising, if controversial venture.
>
> Left far behind are fundamentalists of the 1930-50 era whose pessimistic view of history led them to exclude socio-political involvement and cultural engagement in favor of concentrated personal evangelism in expectation of Christ's imminent return. . . . This viewpoint still has support in Bob Jones circles and in an older Dallas Seminary constituency. . . . Most evangelicals assume we must be strenuously involved in public affairs.[15]

How should we evaluate the efforts of the New Evangelicals to mount social programs in order to address the ills of society? Certainly our modern society has many grievous problems which wrench the heart of a believer. But we must follow Scripture and not our emotions. There is no evidence in the New Testament of any church-sponsored social programs organized for the purpose of alleviating human suffering in the unsaved world. Careful study of the New Testament will reveal that efforts to meet social needs were confined for the most part to believers (Acts 4:32-37). James exhorts us to demonstrate our faith by helping fellow believers who are "naked" or "destitute of daily food" (James 2:15). These and other illustrations show us that the social concern of the early believers was primarily aimed at fellow believers and not at the world in general. This is not to say that individual believers cannot and should not show kindness and generosity to the world's needy. Certainly such behavior is appropriate and reflects the spirit of Christ. But the New Evangelicals, reacting to the drumbeat of criticism coming from the liberals who say fundamentalists have no concern for others, have gone too far in their espousal of social programs. The main work of the churches of Christ is not to minister to outward and physical human needs, but to preach the gospel of the Son of God which speaks to a far deeper and more eternal need—the salvation of the soul. In fairness it should be noted too that fundamentalists through the years have shown kindness and love to sinners in their sin, often combining those acts of kindness with the proclamation of the gospel (such as in the ministry of rescue missions).

Inspiration of Scripture

A willingness to redefine and to reevaluate the church's historic position on the verbal inspiration of Scripture was truly opening a Pandora's box, as can now be seen several generations later. In the original *Christian Life* article, the reopening of the subject of biblical inspiration was described as "just a pebble in the pond of conservative theology" which could "expand to the bombshell of mid-century evangelicalism."[16] Never were truer words spoken! With great rapidity more and more leaders who claim the title "evangelical" have drifted from the time-honored and solid position of biblical inerrancy to some greatly modified position. It is still true that "all scripture [each and every scripture] is given by inspiration of God" (II Tim. 3:16). This includes everything—geographical references, historical references, and scientific references, as well as theological teaching. Years ago Ronald Nash spoke favorably of the shifts in New Evangelical views on bibliology: "If evangelicalism has modified, in any way, the fundamentalist view of inspiration, the modification is a step in the right direction. By that I mean it is a positive step in the direction of a more understandable and defensible position on the inspiration of the Bible."[17]

Nash, however, was wrong. Witness the great liberties now taken by "evangelical" scholars with the text of Scripture. It has

19

become a lump of clay which they may twist into the strangest shapes and then pronounce perfectly normal.

Finally, the New Evangelicals were determined to engage in "meaningful" conversation with liberal theologians. Vernon Grounds, who at that time was president of Conservative Baptist Seminary in Denver, offered this opinion: "An evangelical can be organizationally separated from all Christ-denying fellowship and yet profitably engage in an exchange of ideas with men who are not evangelical."[18] Grounds had the notion that fraternization with Bible-denying scholars would somehow have a positive effect upon those who attempted it.

Part of the problem with many New Evangelicals is that they do not recognize theological liberals as lost souls, groping in spiritual darkness, "wells without water, clouds that are carried with a tempest; to whom the mist of darkness is reserved forever" (II Pet. 2:17). Many evangelicals simply view liberals as misguided but well-meaning Christians who need our love and fellowship. We might thus be able to lead them from their erring ways. Bloesch, while commending some aspects of early fundamentalism, took issue with the great scholar J. Gresham Machen who wrote the classic book, *Christianity and Liberalism.* Machen, in Bloesch's judgment, "did not take adequate recognition of the fact that liberals can still be men of deep personal faith despite the errors in their thinking."[19] But with the men in question, we are talking about far more than merely a few intellectual miscues. We are talking about blatant rebellion against Almighty God and the authority of His holy Word. Bloesch goes on to remark, "Evangelicals should not spurn fellowship with those ecumenists and liberals who confess Jesus Christ as Lord and Savior. Liberalism as a theological system must of course be repudiated, but should we not seek reconciliation with liberals as persons?"[20] But should we indeed? God tells us exactly what we are to do with them—"from such turn away" (II Tim. 3:5). Unfortunately, New Evangelicals are not heeding that warning. Bloesch concludes his discussion of the matter by stating, "It is heartening to discern a new spirit of openness in the breed of evangelicals, many of whom are the children of fundamentalism."[21] This trend, while viewed by some as a step of progress, in the light of biblical revelation can only be viewed as a step of regress.

Special Issue—Ecclesiastical Separation

One of the chief differences between New Evangelicals and fundamentalists concerns the views of each regarding what we call "ecclesiastical separation." Fundamentalist separatists believe that there should be complete separation from all churches and fellowships of churches that tolerate unbelief or compromise with error. In contrasting fundamentalism and evangelicalism, Peterson observed, "The spirit of evangelicalism . . . is more *amiable*. We consider it important to maintain fellowship with other Christians, even if they are mistaken on certain issues, especially if they can join us in advancing the gospel."[22] This observation is quite typical of the general attitude of New Evangelicals—"let us compromise doctrinal matters for the sake of evangelism." More will be said about this at a later time.

Years ago, when the division came between the National Association of Evangelicals and the American Council of Christian Churches, it was evident that there was a deep cleavage over the matter of separation from apostasy. J. Elwin Wright, one of the early leaders of the NAE, explained the NAE position regarding ecclesiastical separation, in his comments on what he conceived as a key passage—II Corinthians 6:17. "I believe . . . that the Corinthian epistle does not at all suggest withdrawal from a church which is plagued by backslidings, heresies, or departure from the doctrines and moral standards of the Word. It does teach that those who are faithful should purge the church of these unbelievers."[23] In further support of his view, Wright called forth witness from the Old Testament when he wrote, "A search of the Old Testament from Genesis to Malachi reveals no single instance of a schismatic movement in Israel which had divine sanction."[24]

Two things need to be noted about Wright's position, which still represents the position of the NAE. He plainly states that even though a body has departed from the "doctrines . . . of the Word" we are not required as Christians to separate from such a body. Second, he defends this position by saying that there was no divinely appointed separation from the nation Israel. Wright failed to recognize the fact that Israel and the church are not the same and that the same principles of fellowship that govern a theocracy do not govern the church of Jesus Christ. The nation Israel was not a voluntary association of believers as is a local church. It was a national, political, and economic entity into which one was physically born. New Testament churches are different in their makeup. They are sovereign entities that have the responsibility of maintaining their own purity as they obey the teachings of the New Testament. Why do men resist the biblical injunctions to break fellowship with those who deny the faith and promote unscriptural positions? Without a doubt, one of the reasons is the fact that taking a stand against unbelief can be very costly. This was well demonstrated in the conflict that arose in some of the denominations years ago. Men had labored for most of their ministry within the bounds of certain denominational affiliations. They had friendships, and, more than that, they had financial investments. They were wedded to denominational pension programs which they would lose if they left the fold. It was too great a price for some to pay.

Perhaps an even stronger reason is the fact that there was a certain prestige and influence to be had in a place of denominational leadership that one would not obtain as an independent outside the organized structure of the denominations. In analyzing the development of the New Evangelicalism, Marsden says that the most explosive issue that faced the emerging New Evangelical leaders was the question of separation from their affiliations. His comments are very perceptive and certainly serve to explain why many men would not separate from the denominations of which they were a part.

> Must they separate from corrupted denominations? Not only were the new evangelicals attempting to reform fundamentalism, they at the same time remained loyal fundamentalists who viewed their more basic mission as the reform of degenerating Protestantism. Were those who witnessed against the grave apostasy of the comfortable, culturally respected churches obliged to separate themselves from the apostasy? . . . Must they get out and become plaintive voices in the wilderness, or could they stay on and work for reform from their more influential positions within?[25]

Influence. Position. Respect. Are these more important than obedience to God? Have there not been many "plaintive voices" down through the centuries, outside the world's sphere of influence and power as well as the ecclesiastical establishment? Was there not a man called Enoch who walked with God without the blessing and approval of his contemporaries? And was there not Noah who managed with the support of only seven people? And what about

Jeremiah who had the audacity to rebuke the sinners of his day and received for his pains open scorn and physical abuse? Consider also the Apostle Paul who labored in weariness, pain, and various perils, and languished in many a prison for Jesus' sake. Or what of that magnificent company of "plaintive voices" who are magnified in Scripture as having been "stoned . . . sawn asunder . . . slain with the sword . . . afflicted" (Heb 11:37), making their homes in the deserts and caves of the land, giving up everything they counted important in life for the sake of the Lord. No positions of "influence" here. They were like the prophet John the Baptist who was a "voice crying in the wilderness," another of those "plaintive voices in the wilderness" so shunned by New Evangelical leaders.

Let us be plain. To stand for truth and righteousness is very costly. Some men have paid a great price to be true to God. Many New Evangelicals today honor Charles Haddon Spurgeon, but if they were true to the philosophy they espouse, none of them would have stood with him when the British Baptist Union voted to excommunicate him from that fellowship because of his militant stand against the apostasy tolerated within. In the "Downgrade Controversy" that rocked the Baptists of Great Britain, even many of Spurgeon's former students stood against him. He had clothed them, put food on their tables, and seen to their ministerial education. Denominational loyalties, however, proved too strong for many of them. Their mentor was too militant. Thus they cast their votes against him and he stood virtually alone. But the hand of God was with him, and his church outshone by far most of those who caved in to the enemies of God. It was D. M. Panton who, many years ago, said, "To identify oneself with the truth is to place one's self in the heart of a storm from which there is no escape for life."

In further exploring the reason that early New Evangelicals steered away from the principle of ecclesiastical separation, we need to note the fact that their concept of the purpose of the church was different from that of fundamentalists. Fundamentalists have generally held what is called the "Donatist" concept of the church over the "Augustinian" view. That is, they place a primary importance upon the *holiness* of the visible church over the *unity* of the visible church. Augustine, an early leader and scholar of the church, fought against the Donatists who were separatists and who would not fellowship with elements of the visible church that they deemed

23

as compromising. Augustine's concern for unity within the church tended to undermine the scriptural goal of purity within the church. Fundamentalist separatists today believe that the purpose of the visible churches is not merely to maintain an outward unity at all costs but to preserve and defend the truth of God and the purity of the body of Christ.

Furthermore, the early evangelical scholars who laid the foundation for the more full-blown movement that was to arise saw the church's mission as one of penetrating the world with Christian values. Fundamentalists, said they, are satisfied merely to win people to Christ and disciple them. This is not sufficient. The church must arise and seek to influence economic, political, and social areas of society with Christian principles. The mission of the church is not confined to the preaching of the gospel and resultant spiritual nourishment, but is expanded to include a responsibility to influence society toward Christian standards. One writer has put it this way:

> The new evangelicals' rejection of separatism as an article of faith was related to their conception of the cultural role of fundamentalism or evangelicalism. They were closer to the heritage of the first Puritan governor of Massachusetts, John Winthrop, who aspired to build a Christian civilization, than they were to the dissident Roger Williams, who demanded a pure separatist church and saw the state as hopelessly secular. . . . The new evangelical reformers put more emphasis, therefore, on . . . cultural transformation.[26]

A careful study of the New Testament will fail to find any commission to the church to attempt a "cultural transformation." The Great Commission of our Lord contains no such command. The prince of darkness is the political and religious head of this world system and will remain so until his total defeat by the Lord Jesus Christ (John 16:11; II Cor 4:4). There is no evidence in the New Testament epistles that the church was to attempt to reform the culture of this world. The Holy Spirit of God today is moving among the nations of earth "to take out of them a people for his name" (Acts 15:14). He is not endeavoring to Christianize the nations.

Trying to Be "Good Guys"

It is fair to say, we believe, that the spirit of the New Evangelicalism is one of compromise, the avoidance of controversy. It is interesting that, in describing the early problems that Fuller Seminary had with the Presbyterian denomination, Marsden reports that the Presbyterians thought the seminary divisive. In seeking to counteract that perception and maintain a good name for themselves with denominational leaders, the leaders of Fuller "side-stepped controversy."[27] New Evangelicals have specialized in "side-stepping controversy." What we need, according to many of these leaders, is not *confrontation,* but *contextualization.* "What is required is not merely a practical application of biblical doctrine but a translation of that doctrine into a conceptuality that meshes with the reality of our social structures and the patterns of life dominant in contemporary life."[28] He seems to be saying that the church should adapt, that it should accommodate. The church should present its message within the acceptable patterns of contemporary society.

Francis Schaeffer was not always a consistent separatist. He began his ministry in the fires of controversy that accompanied the departure of J. Gresham Machen and others from the Presbyterian church. However, he later embraced a much broader fellowship and would not have been known as a strong fundamentalist. In the latter years of his ministry, however, he sounded some very powerful warnings to the church. Particularly did he alert God's people to the dangers of an overly accommodating spirit. Francis Schaeffer's son, Franky, laments what he calls "this pitiful scampering to conform."[29]

Everyone wants to be a "nice guy"; no one wants to be a "bad guy." "Bad guys" are disruptive to cozy fellowships, are theological and ecclesiastical "whistle blowers"—and few want to hear the whistle. As a result of well-meaning efforts on the part of many to be "nice," the cutting edge of Christianity is being dulled. It is certainly correct to say that "evangelical courtesy has seriously watered down its witness," and, realizing that, "we must guard against civility breeding timidity."[30]

Certainly, Christians must repudiate apostate theologians and their supporters. Yet, even some evangelicals balk at this necessity, not wishing to be "offensive" and "triumphal." J. Gresham Machen in 1924 delivered an address at the Founder's Week of the Moody Bible Institute. It was titled "Honesty and Freedom in the Christian Ministry." He said, "The worst sin today is to say that you agree with the Christian faith and believe in the Bible, but then make common cause with those who deny the

25

basic facts of Christianity. Never was it more obviously true that he that is not with Christ is against him."[31]

It is most interesting to read of the conflicts that the great British preacher, Martyn Lloyd-Jones had with those in his own country of Great Britain who wished to tone down the demands of Scripture and compromise with those of various doctrinal persuasions. Lloyd-Jones, who was a strong doctrinal preacher, could not abide those who were weak-kneed in this area. He lamented the rise of a "new breed": "A new climate of opinion has come in very rapidly. . . . So they are utterly impatient with those who demand true doctrine. . . . They have a hearty dislike of the prophets. They want innocuous, harmless men who won't upset anyone at all."[32]

Some New Evangelicals do not hesitate to cross swords with the liberals over the inspiration of Scripture or the deity of Christ. But many do not wish to make dogmatic statements and hold strong positions in areas of doctrine that are disputed among evangelicals. For this reason many will say, "I am not personally a charismatic, but I don't believe in 'bashing' those who hold the charismatic view." There is a spirit of acceptance, a broadness, and a willingness to allow for many variant positions. What has spawned this attitude in the Christian church? "First, it happened because of the degree to which the spirit and attitudes of the world had penetrated the church. It was no accident that evangelicalism began to favor openness and to repudiate 'exclusiveness' at the very period when the prevailing climate of opinion was against dogmatism in every field of knowledge. The contemporary mood was against all absolutes."[33]

This spirit has driven contemporary exegetes to discover all manner of wondrous new teachings buried in the Scripture which no orthodox scholars had ever uncovered until this generation. Lo, and behold, in the name of evangelicalism many now defend homosexuality, abortion, and feminism. How did they come to find these positions? They manufactured them by accommodating the Word of God to the latest intellectual fashions.

Few want to be known as "controversialists." They want to be thought of as loving, kind, and reasonable. One is "reasonable" if one is not dogmatic. This is exactly what one astute observer noted when pondering the gradual weakening of convictions among evangelicals. There is, says he, "an excessive fear of being thought negative, controversial, and belligerent. Criticism of almost any kind has become very unpopular among professing Christians. A loving attitude was thought to be one which accepted everyone for what they appeared to be. . . . The duty of 'contending earnestly for the faith' was put still lower. To emphasize these things was to risk losing the increased acceptance for which evangelicals hoped.' "[34]

There is a tremendous desire among contemporary evangelicals to be accepted by the movers and shakers of this world. They do not want to be viewed as occupying some tiny theological "backwater." They want a place in the sun. Recognition by the world is a burning desire. And many are willing to pay a heavy price to receive such.

One cringes to read the critique of one observer, but its truthfulness must be recognized: "The evangelical community scurries around attempting to curry favor from a secular world that couldn't care less. It manifests itself as pitiful rather than broad-minded, treasonous rather than accommodating . . . willing to abandon even the basic tenets of the faith, such as the inerrancy of Scripture, rather than appear unfashionable."[35] The same writer goes on to say,

> Like peasants shivering in their hovels on the grounds of a magnificent manor house, evangelical leadership often seems to be longing for a place inside the palace—with its bright lights, balloons, and fashionability—or at least to have their doctrinal views validated by the World Council of Churches, or failing that to get published in the *Christian Century.* A pathetic servility, an attempt to always see the other point of view while never defending one's own, and an incessant compromise, embody much of evangelicalism today.[36]

When Fuller Seminary was founded it was touted as an institution of more "open thought." While some early faculty members were not happy with all that that entailed, they soon departed and the seminary went down the road of compromise. In tracing its development, Marsden writes, "The openness necessary to shaping a new evangelical coalition was frankly risky. . . . It also meant that a new emphasis might get out of hand."[37] Well, it certainly got "out of hand." The great radio evangelist, Charles Fuller, would certainly hang his head in shame at the notions that emanate from Fuller Seminary in the name of evangelicalism.

What happens when people compromise vital truth? The institutions, churches, and movements with which they are associated deteriorate spiritually. Even such a one as Thomas Oden, a liberal, sees the danger of accommodation. "The central theme of contemporary theology is accommodation to modernity. . . . The spirit of accommodation has . . . [led to] the steady deterioration of a hundred years and the disaster of the last decades."[38] Early New Evangelical leaders did not envision the lengths to which some of their followers would go in abandoning cherished biblical positions in search for more recognition and better acceptance in a society that despises the demanding and unalterable truths of the Word of God. More and more evangelicals began to "fudge" on the time-honored doctrine of plenary inspiration. In a fascinating study, Schaeffer shows a connection between the original compromise with the apostasy and later compromise with essential doctrine.

> Those who did not leave the liberally-controlled denominations 50 years ago also developed two attitudes. The first was the birth of a general latitudinarianism. . . . If one accepts an ecclesiastical latitudinarianism, it is easy to step into a cooperative latitudinarianism that easily encompasses doctrine, including one's view of Scripture. This is what happened historically. Out of the ecclesiastical latitudinarianism of the thirties and the forties has come the letdown with regard to Scripture in certain areas of evangelicalism in the eighties.[39]

The idea is that the spirit of accommodation which many cultivated within the old apostate denominations from which they refused to separate, has remained with them down through the years. They want no theological battles. They broaden the parameters of theological acceptability as far as they dare to accommodate those who have differing views. Their tent is very large. Hunter is correct when he says that "the symbolic boundaries of Protestant orthodoxy are not being maintained or reinforced."[40] He wonders if contemporary Protestants may now be incapable of defending those boundaries. And to what does he attribute this fearful inability? It has to do with what he calls "the ethic of civility."

> Evangelicals generally and the coming generations particularly have adopted to various degrees an ethical code of political civility. This compels them not only to be *tolerant of others'* beliefs, opinions, and life-styles, but more importantly to be *tolerable to others*. The critical dogma is not to offend but to be

genteel and civil in social relations. While their adoption of this ethic expresses itself politically, it expresses itself as a religious style as well. . . . In this latter sense, it entails a deemphasis of evangelicalism's more offensive aspects, such as accusations of heresy, sin, immorality, and paganism, and themes of judgment, divine wrath, damnation, and hell. Anything that hints of moral or religious absolutism and intolerance is underplayed.[41]

How does this spirit, prevalent in current evangelicalism, square with the Word of God? Did Paul the apostle and other great leaders of the early church seek to accommodate their message to their worldly, unsaved hearers? To the Corinthians he wrote, "And I, brethren, when I came to you, came not with excellency of speech or of wisdom, declaring unto you the testimony of God . . . and my speech and my preaching was not with enticing words of man's wisdom" (I Cor. 2:1, 4). In preaching in Thessalonica Paul did not use "flattering words" (words aimed at making a favorable impression upon them, I Thess. 2:5). He did not mince around but proclaimed the truth plainly and without distortion or attempts to make it "fit" the desires of his hearers (II Cor. 4:1-2). Many were angered with his preaching, so much so that they sought to kill him (Acts 9:23, 29). He readily acknowledged that his plain, unvarnished preaching was "foolishness" to the sophisticated hearer of his day (I Cor. 1:23), but nevertheless vowed that he would not waver for one moment from the proclamation of an unpopular gospel (I Cor. 2:2). Rather than hailing the wisdom of this world as a prize to be desired, he condemned it as "foolishness with God" (I Cor. 3:19). Paul did not set his sails to catch the winds of this world. He proclaimed the truth and relied upon the Holy Spirit to illuminate the minds of his hearers. Paul did not possess the New Evangelical spirit. He was a battler for the faith, wielding the sword of the Spirit against the foes of God.

The Lengthening Shadow of Compromise

The New Evangelicalism, spawned as it was in the minds of brilliant leaders, began immediately to have a broadening influence and to gather to itself many capable exponents. The influence of the New Evangelicalism became powerful indeed. Its tentacles grew until they reached into every major area of evangelical endeavor.

The Mind-Molding of Students

Generally speaking, a person is the product of his education. He is a reflection of the schools which he attended. Many of the original New Evangelical leaders were scholars and leaders in various educational institutions. The value of capturing colleges and seminaries was not lost to them. To perpetuate their principles, they needed to infiltrate the classrooms of Christian schools and thus influence the coming generation of leaders. This they were able to do with remarkable success.

One of the early fountains of New Evangelical thought was Wheaton College, revered by many as a classic example of excellence in Christian higher education. It gradually deteriorated in its position until it harbored on its faculty professors who embraced theistic evolution and other heretical doctrines. It is one of several professedly Christian colleges that became the source for the study put together by James Davison Hunter in his book *Evangelicalism: The Coming Generation.* Basically the book details the liberalizing tendencies which have been at work in many of the recognized evangelical colleges and seminaries for many years. It documents departure from traditional, biblical views on such matters as the family, theology, morality, politics, and education. It is a frightening book, focusing upon information derived from interviews at sixteen liberal arts colleges and seminaries that claim to be evangelical— *Colleges:* Wheaton College, Gordon College, Westmont College, Taylor University, Messiah College, George Fox College, Bethel College, Seattle-Pacific University, and Houghton College; *Seminaries:* Fuller Theological Seminary, Gordon-Conwell Theological Seminary, Westminster Theological Seminary, Asbury Theological Seminary, Talbot Theological Seminary, Wheaton Graduate School, and Conservative Baptist Theological Seminary. Hunter is correct when he observes, "This sample of colleges and seminaries represents higher education at the very heart of American Evangelicalism."[42] Hunter is not approaching his subject as a fundamentalist, but his insights are very telling.

Many years ago, when the New Evangelicalism was not nearly as developed nor as prevalent as it now is, one writer noted, "A growing number of schools that have been known in the past for their stand with fundamentalism now have men on their faculties who speak very highly of neoevangelicalism and teach its principles to the students. The results have been, and will continue to be, devastating."[43]

As one looks over the list of schools studied by Hunter, one's mind drifts back through the years to contemplate the beginnings of some of those schools. Gordon College, for example, had its roots in the Bible institute started by A. J. Gordon, the great fundamentalist pastor and missionary enthusiast. Houghton College was started by conservative holiness people, as was Asbury. Conservative Baptist Seminary of Denver was brought into being as a protest against the liberal institutions of the old Northern Baptist Convention, but it soon began slipping into the New Evangelicalism; many of the men who rejoiced at its birth wept at its deterioration and resigned from its board. Westminster Seminary came into being as a result of the battle of J. Gresham Machen against the liberalism within Presbyterianism.

How could we summarize what Hunter learned from his excursion among the New Evangelical centers of learning? Here is the way he puts it:

> This much is clear, however: conservative Protestantism has changed in significant ways since the beginning of the century, and from all appearances, it is continuing to change. . . . The most important case in point is the place of the Scriptures. When it is allowed, as it is increasingly so in Evangelicalism, to interpret the Bible subjectivistically and to see portions of the Scripture as symbolic or non-binding, the Scriptures are divested of their authority to compel obedience. They may still inspire, but they are substantially disarmed.[44]

In other words, Hunter is saying that evangelical colleges and seminaries are taking a looser view of Scripture. When this begins to happen, the authority of Scripture is undermined and, instead of being the final Word from God, it becomes a grab bag from which anyone can derive support to bolster the latest fashionable opinion.

Evangelicals were bitten with the "academic prestige bug." It can transmit a fatal illness. In evaluating the transformation of fundamentalists into New Evangelicals, some have pinpointed a root cause of the problem—the impact of nonbiblical schools.

> Beyond question, a certain number of young scholars (from evangelical backgrounds) and to a lesser extent pastors who have

taken graduate work at Yale, the University of Chicago, or other leading universities, have reformulated their religious beliefs while at these institutions.

In doing so, they have not always maintained their attachment to evangelical views on the Bible. Seminaries in particular often must make difficult choices in the hiring of faculty from among these well-trained men and women. Spiritual harm can result when someone is hired who retains the name of Evangelical without Evangelicalism's fidelity to an infallible or inerrant Bible.[45]

One Sheet of Dirty Linen

Seminaries traditionally have been the fountainheads of a trained ministry. Regrettably, there are no longer many seminaries that stand for the old-time faith and the orthodox teachings of Scripture. Within the scope of this study we cannot examine in any detail a broad spectrum of seminaries. There is much dirty linen to be examined, but we must limit ourselves to one clear example which will serve to illustrate the point. The example chosen is Fuller Theological Seminary. For a very complete study of the problems at Fuller, one should read the fascinating volume by George Marsden entitled *Reforming Fundamentalism: Fuller Seminary and the New Evangelicalism.* The book develops several points.

(1) Fuller Seminary was started with the specific goal of changing the image and direction of fundamentalism. This writer remembers when it began. He was a student at Bob Jones University at the time. Dr. Bob Jones, Sr., returned from a trip to the West Coast where he had visited with his friend Charles Fuller, the respected radio preacher. Dr. Jones said to his "preacher boys" (ministerial students), "Boys, I just visited with Charlie [Fuller]. He told me that he is going to start a seminary that is going to graduate men who will turn the old apostate denominations around. I told Charlie it wouldn't happen and that he would rue the day when he tried it." I do not recall all of the other things that Dr. Jones said that day, but he was much agitated about the matter. As a young student I did not grasp fully the significance of what he was saying, but he proved to be a prophet.

(2) Tensions developed in the early days at Fuller as the school tried to maintain some measure of rapport with fundamentalists while still pursuing a course of change. Wilbur Smith became a

particular thorn in the sides of those who were endeavoring to make more radical changes. Smith was of the "old school" and became concerned about what he perceived as unhealthy doctrinal trends.

(3) Fundamentalists more and more began to reject the seminary.

(4) Conflicts arose among the faculty over the nature of biblical inspiration and other issues.

(5) Conservative faculty members began to depart. These included men such as Wilbur Smith, Charles Woodbridge, and Harold Lindsell. The major reason behind these resignations was the weakening of the school's position on biblical inerrancy. Lindsell documents the struggle over this in his chapter "The Strange Case of Fuller Theological Seminary" in *The Battle for the Bible*.[46]

(6) The seminary changed its doctrinal statement so as to accommodate those who did not believe that the Bible was without errors. Among the leaders in this group was the founder's own son, Daniel Fuller, who became dean of the faculty. This was the final move that propelled the school ever more leftward in its theological position.

The woeful tale of the demise of Fuller Seminary should serve as a warning to all who wish to liberalize the doctrines of Scripture. Initial compromise only becomes more magnified as time goes on. Some view compromise in theology as a mark of maturity. Wuthnow notes that current evangelical scholars are "less dogmatic in dealing with others holding different views."[47] Without a doubt this is true, but that very attitude has become the undoing of the evangelical movement. We are to "hold fast the form of sound words" (II Tim. 1:13). Vigilance and constant struggle are the only ways to keep the faith. There is a certain militancy that is required if one is to defend the "faith once for all delivered to the saints" (Jude 3; literal trans.).

One of the saddest illustrations of how far the tides of compromise can carry a scholar is found in the case of Bernard Ramm. Because Ramm was nurtured in a strong fundamentalist environment as a young man, his early works were helpful (such as *Protestant Biblical Interpretation*). But, carried along with the desire to be academically acceptable, Ramm drifted further and further from a solid theological position. How startling it was to peruse his volume entitled *After Fundamentalism* published in 1983 and find him defending the theological system of Karl Barth, who rejected the inerrancy of Scripture along with other cardinal doctrines. "How are the mighty fallen!"

Going Down the Middle of the Road

To propagate thoughts requires the written page. New Evangelicals were quick to seize upon the medium of writing in order to spread their message. There were many capable scholars and writers among them, and there were publishing houses aplenty ready to publish their works. One of the early and significant steps in the spreading of the New Evangelical gospel was the founding of the magazine *Christianity Today*. Harold Ockenga and Billy Graham, assisted by wealthy Presbyterian layman J. Howard Pew, brought into existence this periodical which was to become the leading voice of the New Evangelicalism. In discussing the founding of the magazine, Billy Graham suggested to Harold Lindsell that Carl Henry, under consideration for the position of editor, might be too fundamentalistic. Marsden, in analyzing correspondence between Graham and Lindsell and citing excerpts, wrote,

> The new periodical, as Graham envisioned it, would "plant the evangelical flag in the middle of the road, taking a conservative theological position but a definite liberal approach to social problems. It would combine the best in liberalism and the best in fundamentalism without compromising theologically." It would see good as well as bad in the World and National Council of Churches. More specifically, "Its view of Inspiration would be somewhat along the line of the recent book by Bernard Ramm [*The Christian View of Science and the Scripture*] which in my opinion does not take away from Inspiration, but rather gives strong support to our faith in the inspiration of the Scriptures."[48]

The phrase "the middle of the road" was, and is, very apropos for the proponents of the New Evangelicalism. The original strategy was to emphasize commonality with ecumenical leaders and thus gain a wider hearing for the magazine. To his credit, Carl Henry did not agree with this approach; nevertheless, as time went on, this was the general thrust of the magazine. In early issues two key editorials appear: "Dare We Revive the Modernist-Fundamentalist Conflict?" (10 June 1957) and "Dare We Renew the Controversy?" (24 June 1957). These editorials expressed a growing impatience with any effort to perpetuate the debate between liberalism and fundamentalism. Another editorial determined that the magazine would "largely be positive and constructive rather than negative and destructive."[49] Thus the pages of *Christianity Today* have regularly reflected this philosophy, a repudiation of militancy against the apostasy and its ecumenical promoters.

Many of the early New Evangelicals were prolific writers. Such men as Carl Henry, Bernard Ramm, Edward J. Carnell, Vernon Grounds, and Harold Ockenga produced numerous books. Carnell in particular became very vitriolic against fundamentalism and poured out his hatred in *The Case for Orthodoxy*. A weak position on biblical inspiration was set forth in Dewey Beegle's *The Inspiration of Scripture*. An attempt was made by Robert Ferm to defend Billy Graham's practice of ecumenical evangelism in his publication *Cooperative Evangelism*. Mention was made earlier of Carl Henry's book *The Uneasy Conscience of Modern Fundamentalism* in which he made a case for greater social involvement on the part of evangelicals. His volume *Remaking the Modern Mind* was also a significant production of the time. Bernard Ramm attempted to adjust scriptural teaching to current scientific views in his work *Christian View of Science and Scripture*.

All these works have certain characteristics in common. First of all, the academic credentials and abilities of the authors were evident. They were widely read and knowledgeable. This gave their writings great credibility, especially among younger evangelicals who felt that fundamentalism lacked academic respectability. In many of their works, the early New Evangelicals give considerable credence to the writings of the enemies of Christianity. This trend has continued to the present hour. New Evangelical works are filled with footnotes and bibliographies drawing upon liberal and neo-orthodox writers but are notably deficient in references to the works of solid fundamentalists. This is part of a constant effort to mold the Christian faith to fit a modern context. It is that process which is now being called "contextualization" by some, that is, the effort to "modernize" the message and methods of the church to make them fit more comfortably with the surrounding culture of our day.

The Impact of Parachurch Organizations

New Evangelicalism was not only permeating the organized churches but also spreading through the medium of various interdenominational groups, some of which were quite influential. One such organization was Bill Bright's Campus Crusade. Bright was a student at Fuller Theological Seminary when he became concerned about the spiritual needs of college students and started working among them. He never finished seminary but left in 1951 to found his organization. Through the years the Crusade members have had close connections with Fuller Seminary and have imbibed much of its position. In Bright's book *Revolution Now,* he declares that Christ was the greatest revolutionary ever and invites His followers to enlist in a strategy that will help to change the world. A film produced by the Crusade bears that very title—*Come Help Change the World.* This seems to ignore the plain biblical teaching that the church's mission is not to change the world, but to preach the gospel and thus gather people out of the world to be the bride for Christ. The Crusade has had a close tie-in with Billy Graham's ecumenical evangelistic crusades, and many noted New Evangelicals have served on the board of Campus Crusade, men such as Harold Ockenga, Mark Hatfield, and Dan Fuller. A former worker in the Campus Crusade characterized their ministry:

> One reason why the Campus Crusade message is so popular is that Campus Crusaders are taught not to use "Christian jargon" like *witness, repent, converted, blood, hell, sin, saved, holiness,* and *apostasy.* . . . Most students and staff members of Campus Crusade with whom I have associated steadfastly refuse to leave apostate churches and denominations. . . . In all of the Campus Crusade meetings I have attended, I do not recall ever hearing baptism mentioned even once. . . . It seems to look upon the local church as a poor, struggling body that desperately needs the life-giving breath of Crusade's super-animated programs and methodology.[50]

Other groups representing the New Evangelical spirit would be Inter-Varsity and World Vision. Countless other lesser-known groups could be added to the number.

One of the strongest mediums for the propagation of New Evangelical principles has been the National Association of Evangelicals. Founded in 1942, it has become an organizational voice for leaders of the New Evangelical movement. While the organization of the NAE antedated the visible rise of the New Evangelicalism, the New Evangelicals, when they did begin to appear, approved of and promoted the NAE. The various denominations included in the NAE will give some idea of the theological inclusiveness of the organization. Some of the member groups are the following:

The Baptist General Conference
Assemblies of God
Christian and Missionary Alliance
Evangelical Free Church
Church of God
The Wesleyan Church
International Pentecostal Holiness Church
Free Methodist Church

The membership is heavily weighted with holiness and Pentecostal bodies. In fact, it is membership in the NAE that has given many of these bodies a respectability in the evangelical community that they did not have prior to their identification.

The NAE has broad ecumenical tendencies both at the national level and through its regional affiliates. Virgil Law, speaking as the leader of the Washington Association of Evangelicals, declared that "evangelicals sometimes find they have more in common with the liberal Protestants they abandoned 40 years ago than with the fundamentalist brothers."[51] He goes on to observe that "evangelicals are warming to liberals."[52]

The NAE took a definite position against ecclesiastical separation. Its first president, Harold Ockenga, who at that time was pastor of the Park Street Church in Boston, explained his convictions in this manner: "The strategy of the fundamentalist was wrong. He had raised a shibboleth of having a pure church, both as a congregation and a denomination. The exegesis of II Corinthians 6:14-18 and the parable of the tares was the basis for his ecclesiology. The sad practice called 'come-outism' developed. The belief that one should have and would find a pure church on earth caused fragmentation."[53]

The NAE was to be characterized by an irenic and cooperative spirit. It makes efforts to be as inclusive as possible. It truly is the "new evangelical coalition."[54] While the leaders in the founding of the NAE were predominantly of a Calvinistic persuasion, they saw the opportunity to promote cooperation between widely diverse groups without, in their judgment, sacrificing individual convictions. Thus the title of the first definitive history of the group was *Cooperation Without Compromise*. The NAE has many affiliated organizations. One of these is the National Religious Broadcasters. One of the chief reasons for the original organization of the NRB was the conflict over religious broadcasting. The Federal Council of Churches (forerunner of the contemporary National Council of Churches) had persuaded major networks to refuse to sell time to religious broadcasters on the plea that this would cut down on "religious racketeering." In fact, however, the fundamentalist broadcasters were reaching a far greater audience than the leaders of the apostasy could tolerate and they sought to put a stop to it. The curtailment of religious broadcasting was a part of their war against fundamentalism. The NRB was organized in 1944 to protect the rights of evangelical broadcasters and enable them to remain on the air. The NRB now includes a wide spectrum of religious radio and television persons and groups (largely New Evangelical) and has reached beyond the continental United States to include persons from other countries.

Contaminating the Great Commission

New Evangelicalism has had a worldwide impact through various missionary organizations as well as worldwide conferences attended by persons from many countries. Thus the problem of New Evangelicalism is not confined to the United States, but will be faced by missionaries the world over.

One of the early factors in the worldwide spread of New Evangelical principles was the World Congress on Evangelism held in Berlin in 1966. Billy Graham was the main motivator behind this congress. Much information concerning it can be found in the large two-volume work *One Race, One Gospel, One Task*, edited by Carl Henry and Stanley Mooneyham. Carl McIntire, fundamentalist leader, was denied entrance even though he had press credentials. However, Oral Roberts, the Pentecostal leader, was welcomed with open arms. It was the first of a number of such international meetings which served to infect large numbers of leaders from other countries with the virus of New Evangelicalism. In 1969 the United States Congress on Evangelism met in Minneapolis. About five thousand were in attendance and were addressed by Billy Graham and others. There was an emphasis upon social action.

Key '73 was another link in the chain of ecumenical missionary endeavors. It was a simultaneous, continent-wide effort to evangelize towns and communities. There were 130 participating church groups. The Executive Committee was composed of Presbyterians, American Baptists, Methodists, Southern Baptists, Anglicans, and others. Its theme was "Calling Our Continent to Christ." The idea for the effort was born in a special meeting in the Marriott Key Bridge Motor Hotel in Arlington, Virginia, in 1967. This so-called Key Bridge Consultation was led by Billy Graham and Carl Henry and included about forty leaders. They decided to develop some plan for confronting every individual in North America with the gospel. While it was a noble goal, its method of accomplishment was decidedly ecumenical. Leaders from some of the most apostate denominations, such as the United Methodist Church, participated. Roman Catholic groups became involved as well. Consider the explanation of the Catholic bishops in Missouri as they called the faithful to participation:

> We, the Catholic Bishops of Missouri, are happy to announce to you that, on behalf of our Catholic people we have accepted an invitation to join in the program known as Key '73. . . .
>
> It will be pervaded with a spirit of genuine ecumenism. . . . Among the means of fostering our personal renewal with Christ are a whole-hearted participation in Christ's offering of Himself in the Mass, deep devotion to Christ present in the Eucharist, personal meeting with Christ the Healer and Reconciler in the Sacrament of Penance . . . use of the Rosary. . . . We shall endeavor to deepen our devotion and loyalty to our most Holy Father, Pope Paul VI.[55]

Little regard was paid to the differences between apostates and believers. One brochure said, "Key '73 is one hopeful sign that the battles between a defunct fundamentalism and a lifeless liberalism are now being left behind, to be fought only by those who wish to live in the past."[56] This statement of course only embodied wishful thinking, namely, that fundamentalism and liberalism are dead and that we should move on to bigger and better things. In fact, there is still a deadly struggle between error, as embodied in liberalism, and truth, as embodied in fundamentalism.

In 1974 a further step was taken to enlarge the scope of the New Evangelicalism worldwide. The International Congress on World Evangelization was held in Lausanne, Switzerland. Again a very

39

ecumenical spirit prevailed. Billy Graham was the honorary chairman. Others on the planning committee included Bill Bright, Leighton Ford, Don Hoke, Harold Lindsell, Stan Mooneyham, and Clyde Taylor. Graham and Carl Henry spoke, as well as Malcolm Muggeridge, Ralph Winter, George Peters, René Padilla, Donald McGavran, John Stott, and others. It was certainly, as one called it, "A Consortium of Compromise." About two-fifths of the evangelicals who attended belonged to churches which were affiliated with the World Council of Churches. Billy Graham reaffirmed the fact that he had "warm relationships" with the World Council and desired that to continue. The concept of ecumenical evangelism was pushed strongly.

The meeting at Lausanne gave great impetus to what has been called the "ethnotheological" or "contextualization" approach to the work of foreign missions. One of the subcommittees was "The Lausanne Consultation on Gospel and Culture," chaired by John Stott. He commented that "only . . . as a result of the Lausanne Congress on World Evangelization in 1974 has the evangelical constituency as a whole come to acknowledge the central importance of culture for the effective communication of the Gospel."[57] This is a most significant statement indeed. Should "culture" have "central" importance in communicating the gospel? This is certainly a departure from the traditional (and, we believe, scriptural) view of missions. We are not to adapt ourselves to men. Men are to submit themselves to God. God does not have a message that is to be shaped by the cultures of men. He has a message which offers an ultimatum to lost creatures that they must repent and turn to Him.

What is meant by "contextualization"? One has said that it "gives preference, as the point of departure for systematic theological thinking, to the contemporary historical scene over against the biblical tradition."[58] In other words, one tries to fit the message to the people and their thinking rather than calling them to accept the thought patterns of Scripture. McGavran, the "high priest" of the "Church Growth Movement" made this astounding observation: "The great obstacles to conversion are social, not theological. Great turning of Moslems and Hindus can be expected as soon as ways are found for them to become Christian without renouncing their brethren, which seems to them a betrayal."[59]

40

The Scriptures specifically state that the obstacle to conversion is theological. Man is dead in his sins (Eph. 2:1), and he is absolutely blind to spiritual truth (II Cor. 4:3-4). He has no desire for God (Rom. 3:11); he is afflicted with hardness of heart (Rom. 2:5). All the cultural adjustments in the world will not overcome these conditions. Only a mighty work of God's Spirit through the preaching of the gospel will accomplish a change!

Out of Lausanne I (in contrast to a later Lausanne II), the heralded "Lausanne Covenant" came. It was a fifteen-point statement which was supposed to express an "evangelical consensus" on certain key areas of doctrine and practice. There were two areas of note. One had to do with the Scriptures. The statement said, "We affirm the divine inspiration, truthfulness and authority of both Old and New Testament Scriptures in their entirety as the only written Word of God, without error in all it affirms, and the only infallible rule of faith and practice."[60] The wording was created in order to satisfy New Evangelicals (such as those of Fuller Seminary) who hold the position that the Bible does not "affirm" (teach with infallible authority) such things as geographical, scientific, or historical details but only doctrine that is essential to salvation. The other area related to the Holy Spirit. The statement exhorted Christians to pray for a special visitation of the Holy Spirit so that "all his gifts may enrich the body of Christ."[61] This was included to accommodate charismatics who attended in large numbers. One of the saddest commentaries on the present condition of evangelicalism was the remarks made in a published article by the president of one of the most prestigious evangelical seminaries in America, one that would be thought fundamentalist by many. An invited participant, he came to the conclusion that we ought not to criticize those who are trying to evangelize even though we might not agree with their methods. As a member of the Independent Fundamental Churches of America, he wrote an article for their official publication. (It should be noted in fairness that many members of that organization did not agree with his conclusions.) The author said,

> It seems to this writer that the challenge that faces us in the IFCA is not the question as to whether or not the Lausanne Conference was all that it should be. . . . The real problem that faces us is the question of what we as a movement and as individuals and churches are willing to do in a constructive way to get the gospel to every creature. Until we are completely committed to the task

of world evangelism ourselves, we should not criticize others who are making an honest attempt in this direction.[62]

Unfortunately, the observation just cited is typical of the response of many evangelicals to compromising programs of this sort. It lacks the militant exposure of error that should be found in a Christian leader's analysis of such a hodgepodge of theological views as was found at the Lausanne conference. The author of this book wrote this Christian leader at the time. Parts of the letter are here quoted because it speaks to some very important matters which Christians need to face.

I have just completed reading your article in the March-April issue of *Voice* on the subject of the Lausanne Congress on World Evangelism. I was deeply disappointed in the article. It contained no real exposure of the subtle dangers and open compromises of this gathering which had first been manifested in the Berlin Congress several years ago. You did mention the fact that there were those there whose theological orthodoxy could be questioned, but you did not attach the importance to this that I believe the Scriptures do. Certainly this kind of "mixed multitude" does not represent in any manner the historic position of the IFCA as I understand it. To me it would seem that the challenge that faces the IFCA does directly relate to the question "as to whether or not the Lausanne Conference was all it should be."

This is a very key issue. Whether or not there were persons assembled there who had a heart for world missions and a concern for lost people is beside the point. The issue is whether or not this concern was expressed within a biblical framework. I believe that it was not. . . .

The kind of compromised position represented at Lausanne should be thoroughly exposed by those in places of leadership and influence. Many of us are "completely committed to the task of world evangelism" and we therefore believe that we have the right and scriptural duty to criticize those who are endeavoring to evangelize in an unbiblical context.[63]

The liberal *Christian Century* had this comment on Lausanne: "Moreover, the 'Lausanne Covenant,' a concise but broadly based affirmation of evangelical faith and witness, made clear that many conservative Protestants were ready to shed the fundamentalist baggage that had prevented them from participating fully in the life of the world-wide church."[64]

In 1989 a second International Congress on World Evangelization was convened in Manila. Billy Graham was also the one who provided the impetus for this assembly. It was called by some a "Global Camp Meeting." It included a wide variety of persons from many different backgrounds and theological perspectives. At least three issues were prominent:

1. Could charismatics and noncharismatics work together?
2. To what extent would evangelical missions include social ministry?
3. How would people respond to the growing voice of the "Third World" church?

Leighton Ford was the chairman of the congress. The attendees spanned every major denomination from Roman Catholic to evangelical and from mainline Protestant to charismatic. Some called it the largest cross-cultural and cross-denominational gathering ever held.

The first of the above-mentioned three issues was especially important. The charismatics were present in large numbers. Jack Hayford, a Pentecostal pastor from California, issued a strong plea for all evangelicals to be open to the manifestation of miraculous "signs and wonders." The church will grow, he claimed, as it experiences "signs and wonders."

There was a large emphasis upon the social involvement of Christians. Many felt that the "Manila Manifesto," released as an official statement from the congress, was too heavily reflective of liberation theology. At its *best,* liberation theology stresses the need for correcting the social ills of the world through the efforts of the church. To liberation theologians, salvation is to be equated with social and political transformation. At its *worst,* liberation theology is a violent, revolutionary social movement tinged with Marxism.

Many rejoiced at the broadness evidenced in the meeting. "Moreover, the conference manifested a remarkable sense of unity as charismatics and noncharismatics joined hands and worshipped together, and Roman Catholics and Orthodox were welcomed as participants and treated as equals."[65] The same observer noted, "Another important development was Lausanne's softening of its hitherto hard-line stance toward the World Council of Churches. An olive branch was extended to the ecumenical movement."[66]

Richard Heldenbrand investigates the impact of New Evangelicalism upon missions in his insightful volume *Christianity and New Evangelical Philosophies.* Evaluating particularly the impact of Charles Kraft and Eugene Nida upon the work of missions, Heldenbrand notes that their work has had an adverse effect. At the time Kraft was a professor at Fuller Theological Seminary and Nida was Secretary for Translations of the American Bible Society. They propounded an approach to Bible translation and to the proclamation of the gospel message that said that the most important consideration is whether the hearer understands the message rather than whether the message is accurate. "The older focus in translating was the form of the message. . . . The new focus, however, has shifted from the form of the message to the response of the receptor."[67]

While we certainly desire translations that will be understood by the common man, we must ever be watchful that the translation conveys the actual meaning of the original text. If we do not do that, the Scriptures become a lump of clay which the translator may mold at his will. The emphasis must always be upon the message since it is God's message and must not be tampered with in any way. "The prophet that hath a dream, let him tell a dream; and he that hath my word, let him speak my word faithfully. . . . Is not my word like as a fire? saith the Lord; and like a hammer that breaketh the rock in pieces?" (Jer. 23:28-29).

Looking Through the Lens of Scripture

How should one evaluate the New Evangelicalism in the light of Scripture? It should first be noted that the principle of accommodation is not taught in the New Testament. We are not to trim the message or the methods of God in order to win a hearing for our message. The servant of God is to be "rightly dividing the word of truth" (II Tim. 2:15). Some have suggested the rendering "cutting a straight course" in the Word of truth, and still others have rendered the word "correctly handling." The point is that we are not to seek to conform God's Word to man's desires. We are not to be "conformed to this world" (Rom. 12:2), or, as some have suggested, "Do not allow the world to pour you into its mold."

While an ecumenical spirit seems to some to be brotherly and kind, it is not in line with God's instructions for a believer. Often the concept that lies behind this approach is the preeminence of love over doctrine. Ecumenists sometimes appeal to John 17:11, where Jesus prays "that they may be one." They excoriate Christians who oppose the ecumenical movement, accusing them of not obeying this command and perpetuating the "sin of division." We need to be reminded, however, that this request of our Lord has been answered already, and believers are one in the body of Christ (I Cor. 12:13; Eph. 2:22). The verse does not deal with organizational unity but with spiritual unity. To seek organizational unity at the expense of doctrinal compromise is wrong. Paul specifically writes, "Now I beseech you, brethren, mark them which cause divisions and offences contrary to the doctrine which ye have learned; and avoid them" (Rom. 16:17).

An aspect of New Evangelicalism that especially concerns fundamentalists is its permeation by charismatic theology. The founders of New Evangelicalism were not themselves charismatic, but they have given it a new respectability by their insistence that we should accept charismatic doctrine as a viable option rather than denounce it as an unbiblical error. It seems to this author that we must say two things: (1) The charismatics are wrong in their views of the Holy Spirit and His work. (2) Their position should be rejected and Christian people should be taught that charismatic theology and practice are contrary to the teaching of Scripture. This approach to the movement, however, is not popular with the modern evangelicals. It is too confrontational, too divisive, and too unloving.

It is not within the scope of this book to discuss the theological shortcomings of the charismatics.[68] Paul is plain as to our duty as pastors and Christian leaders: "Holding fast the faithful word as he hath been taught, that he may be able by sound doctrine both to exhort and to convince the gainsayers" (Titus 1:9). That is the positive part of the ministry. The negative part is equally as important. In speaking of those who teach incorrect doctrine, Paul says, "Wherefore rebuke them sharply, that they may be sound in the faith" (Titus 1:13). It is not a mark of graciousness to allow false teaching to be propagated.

New Evangelicalism has done great harm. It has become pervasive in evangelical circles. It has weakened the biblical foundations of many churches and organizations and has emphasized the pragmatic over the theological. In our next chapter, we must turn

45

to a study of the one man who, more than any other, popularized this approach—Evangelist Billy Graham.

Notes

[1] Harold Lindsell, *The Bible in the Balance*, p. 320.

[2] Sherman Roddy, "Fundamentalists and Ecumenicity," *Christian Century*, 1 October 1958, p. 1110.

[3] Vernon Grounds, "Fundamentalism and Evangelicalism: Legitimate Labels or Illicit Libels?" Printed by Conservative Baptist Theological Seminary, Denver.

[4] George Marsden, "From Fundamentalism to Evangelicalism: A Historical Analysis," in *The Evangelicals*, edited by David Wells and John Woodbridge.

[5] Richard Quebedeaux, *The Worldly Evangelicals*, p. 85.

[6] Letter from Edward J. Carnell to the constituency of Fuller Theological Seminary.

[7] Arnold Hearn, "Fundamentalist Renaissance," *Christian Century*, 30 April 1958, p. 528.

[8] Harold Ockenga, "Resurgent Evangelical Leadership," *Christianity Today*, 10 October 1960, p. 13.

[9] Carl Henry, "YFC's 'Cheer for Jesus' No Substitute for the Apostles' Creed," *World*, 11 March 1990.

[10] George Marsden, *Reforming Fundamentalism*, p. 63.

[11] Ibid.

[12] George Marsden, *Understanding Fundamentalism and Evangelicalism*, p. 67.

[13] Ibid., pp. 71-72.

[14] James D. Hunter, *Evangelicalism: The Coming Generation*, p. 33.

[15] Carl F. H. Henry, "The New Coalitions," *Christianity Today*, 17 September 1989, p. 26.

[16] "Is Evangelical Theology Changing?" *Christian Life*, March 1956.

[17] Ronald Nash, *The New Evangelicalism*, p. 42.

[18] "Is Evangelical Theology Changing?" *Christian Life*, March 1956, p. 19.

[19] Donald Bloesch, *The Evangelical Renaissance*, p. 149.

[20] Ibid., p. 150.

[21] Ibid.

[22] J. Randall Peterson, "Evangelicalism: A Movement's Direction," *Evangelical Newsletter*, 20 December 1985, p. 4.

[23]J. Elwin Wright, "The Issue of Separation," *United Evangelical Action,* 15 August 1945, p. 13.

[24]Ibid.

[25]Marsden, *Reforming Fundamentalism,* pp. 6-7.

[26]Ibid., pp. 7-8.

[27]Ibid., pp. 6-7.

[28]David Wells, "An American Evangelical Theology: The Painful Transition from Theoria to Praxis," in *Evangelicalism and Modern America,* edited by George Marsden, p. 90.

[29]Franky Schaeffer, *Bad News for Modern Man,* p. 45.

[30]David Neff, "The Down Side of Civility," *Christianity Today,* 6 February 1987, p. 13.

[31]*Christian Beacon,* 17 January 1957.

[32]Ian Murray, *David Martyn Lloyd-Jones: The Fight of Faith,* p. 504.

[33]Ibid., p. 666.

[34]Ibid., p. 444.

[35]Schaeffer, p. 67.

[36]Ibid., p. 68.

[37]Marsden, *Reforming Fundamentalism,* pp. 266-67.

[38]Francis A. Schaeffer, p. 100.

[39]Francis A. Schaeffer, interview, "Schaeffer Reflects on 50 years of Denominational Ins and Outs," *Christianity Today,* 10 April 1981, p. 29.

[40]Hunter, p. 183.

[41]Ibid.

[42]Ibid., p. 9.

[43]Robert Ligthner, *Neoevangelicalism Today,* p. 171.

[44]Hunter, p. 184.

[45]John Woodbridge, Mark Noll, Nathan Hatch, *The Gospel in America,* p. 130.

[46]Harold Lindsell, "The Strange Case of Fuller Theological Seminary," in *The Battle for the Bible,* pp. 106-21.

[47]Robert Wuthnow, *The Struggle for America's Soul,* p. 175.

[48]Marsden, *Reforming Fundamentalism,* p. 158.

[49]Editorial, "On Meeting Changing Issues," *Christianity Today,* 4 March 1957, p. 20.

[50]Charles Dunn, "Campus Crusade: Its Message and Methods," *Faith for the Family,* October 1980, pp. 3, 18-19.

[51]John McCoy, "Evangelical Churches Have Foot in Each Camp," *Seattle Post-Intelligencer,* 22 February 1986, p. 6.

[52]Ibid.

[53]Harold Ockenga, "From Fundamentalism Through New Evangelicalism to Evangelicalism," in *Evangelical Roots,* edited by Kenneth Kantzer, p. 42.

[54]Joel Carpenter, "The Fundamentalist Leaven and the Rise of an Evangelical United Front," in *The Evangelical Tradition in America,* edited by Leonard Sweet, p. 283.

[55]M. H. Reynolds, "Key '73: An Appraisal," p. 22.

[56]Ibid., p. 35.

[57]John R. W. Stott, "Foreword" to *Down to Earth,* edited by John R. W. Stott and Robert Coote, p. vii.

[58]Nikos A. Nissiotis, Circular letter, October 1970.

[59]Donald McGavran, *Understanding Church Growth,* p. 310.

[60]John Millheim, "A Consortium of Compromise," *Baptist Bulletin,* October 1974.

[61]Ibid.

[62]John F. Walvoord, "The Lausanne Congress on Evangelism," *Voice,* March-April 1975, p. 22.

[63]Personal letter from Ernest Pickering to John F. Walvoord.

[64]Richard Pierard, "Lausanne II: Reshaping World Evangelicalism," *Christian Century,* 16-23 August 1989, p. 740.

[65]Ibid.

[66]Ibid.

[67]Eugene Nida and Charles Taber, *The Theory and Practice of Translation,* p. 1.

[68]Some basic errors of the charismatic movement may be summarized as follows: (1) a failure to recognize that New Testament miracles were confined to the apostolic era, (2) the elevation of a minor gift (tongues) to a place of prominence, (3) a lack of differentiation between permanent and temporary spiritual gifts, (4) a misunderstanding of the original purpose of the gift of tongues, and (5) an emphasis on an experience-centered faith as opposed to a theologically centered faith. For further information on the charismatic movement, consult the following works: Victor Budgen, *Charismatics and the Word of God;* Thomas R. Edgar, *Miraculous Gifts: Are They for Today?;* Robert Gromacki, *The Modern Tongues Movement;* John F. MacArthur, *Charismatic Chaos;* and Ernest D. Pickering, *Charismatic Confusion.*

Broadening the Sawdust Trail

Ecumenical Evangelism and Billy Graham

Strange as it may seem, the New Evangelical movement began to soar on the wings of evangelism. The practice of "ecumenical evangelism," which harnessed the forces of churches of widely varying theological persuasions, became the engine which gave popular impetus to the movement.

Evangelicalism and Evangelism

Bible-believing Christians have always taken seriously the command of Christ to evangelize the world. Even in the midst of terrific cultural and theological pressure, believers in the Middle Ages witnessed to the truth. The rulers of the Roman Catholic church hounded them mercilessly, but they continued to preach the gospel over the continent of Europe. It was a concern for the purity of the gospel that fueled the Reformation, Luther insisting that salvation was by faith alone without the ecclesiastical trappings that had clouded it. The great missionary awakening which sent the gospel into pagan lands was certainly evidence of the concern of many for the salvation of the lost.

In England and America great evangelistic movements have sprung up. Under the powerful preaching of George Whitefield, multitudes were converted. Later D. L. Moody took the gospel to the great cities of America in the form of large campaigns. This style continued under such noted evangelists as R. A. Torrey, Bob Jones, Sr., and J. Wilbur Chapman. Billy Sunday, colorful city-wide evangelist, exhorted thousands to "hit the sawdust trail," and they streamed down those aisles of sawdust under the cover of the large tabernacles erected for Sunday's campaigns.

Bible institutes (later Bible colleges) such as the Moody Bible Institute were founded with the principal aim to train young people to win others to Christ. Schools such as Bob Jones University and

John Brown University were founded by evangelists. Charles E. Fuller and others blanketed the air waves with the gospel of Christ. Rescue missions such as the Pacific Garden Mission in Chicago became lighthouses for Christ amidst the skid rows of America.

If there was one activity that was close to the heart of evangelicals the world over, it was evangelism. This is not to say that all were fiery witnesses, but truly born-again people seemed to have a special place in their hearts for the work of getting out the gospel. Tragically, it was at this very point that they were waylaid into adopting a method of evangelism which was contrary to the Word of God. Their fervent interest in evangelism caused many of them to be taken in by the new methodology. It sounded so appealing and seemed so successful. Who would ever be so unspiritual as to challenge an evangelist or his evangelism? To do so seemed to many to be sacrilege. Are we not in this world to evangelize? If someone is evangelizing, winning large numbers to Christ, ought not we to support him? Such was the thinking (and remains the thinking) of many. What happened to cause this confusion and conflict within the church of Christ?

Starting Down the Slippery Edge

One man appeared upon the American evangelistic scene who forever changed the approach of many churches toward evangelism. His name was Billy Graham. There is no doubt that he almost single-handedly popularized the cause and principles of the New Evangelicalism and made it a success. Harold Ockenga, whom we have already identified as perhaps the "father" of New Evangelicalism, stated without hesitation that Billy Graham was "the spokesman of the convictions and ideals of the new evangelicalism."[1] In 1958 while still a young man, Graham was called "the maturing leader of an important new movement in modern Christianity. . . . Graham stands in the forefront of a new evangelical community."[2]

I remember the young Billy Graham. In the 1940s he was a popular speaker with Youth for Christ and used to visit my alma mater periodically. Tall, gangly, and good-looking, he was immediately recognized on the campus when he appeared.

Since Bob Jones University has taken much "flak" over its opposition to Graham's evangelistic philosophy, it is interesting to note that in his early fundamentalist days, Graham was not only a student at the University but also a great admirer of its founder, Bob Jones, Sr. In 1944 he wrote to Bob Jones, Jr., and said, "I want you to be personally assured of my love and loyalty to you, Dr. Bob Senior, and all that Bob Jones College stands for." Later in October of 1950, Billy wrote to Bob Jones, Sr., and said, "Please believe me also, I need your advice and counsel and covet your long years of experience to help guide me across the many pitfalls. Modernists are beginning to write letters against me. . . . All of us young evangelists look up to you as a father."[3]

Graham's associations and his ministry were within the fundamentalist movement at that time. The great fundamentalist patriarch, W. B. Riley, pastor of the First Baptist Church of Minneapolis, had founded the Northwestern Schools in that city. Relinquishing the reins of leadership at those institutions, Riley personally chose Billy Graham to succeed him in the presidency. Graham lasted about three and a half years in this capacity, but he never felt comfortable with the office. The Northwestern Schools encountered financial difficulties and finally closed for a time, reopening later on another campus in a suburb of St. Paul. The college fell into the hands of New Evangelicals and has continued in that vein. The seminary which Riley founded, and over which Graham presided for a time, was moved into the facilities of the Fourth Baptist Church of Minneapolis, pastored by Richard Clearwaters, was renamed Central Baptist Theological Seminary, and continues to be a fundamentalist, separatist institution.

Graham began to be featured in city-wide crusades and, for a time, was sponsored by fundamentalist churches. While Graham was editor-in-chief of W. B. Riley's magazine, *The Pilot,* the masthead proclaimed a "militant stand against Modernism in every form." He was on the Cooperating Board of *The Sword of the Lord,* a strong, fundamentalist paper edited by John R. Rice. He was a personal friend of Bob Jones, Sr., and Bob Jones, Jr., and was honored by Bob Jones University with a doctor's degree. Bob Shuler, great fundamentalist pastor of the Trinity Methodist Church in Los Angeles, and friend of Graham's, wrote in the *Methodist Challenge,* "None of the great evangelists had ever before accepted the sponsorship of modernists. Billy himself had not only refused to hold a campaign under their sponsorship but had openly declared that he never would. *In his Los Angeles campaign, I personally saw and heard him decline the approval and cooperation of the Church Federation which represented the Federal Council, now the National Council."*[4]

Billy Graham was for many years a fundamentalist. He was supported by fundamentalists. He spoke in fundamentalist gatherings and aided fundamentalist enterprises. But something happened; something changed. What was it that propelled the young evangelist from being a fundamentalist to becoming the acknowledged leader of the New Evangelicalism?

Several incidents began to alarm fundamentalist leaders and cause them to wonder what was happening to Graham. He publicly endorsed the Revised Standard Version of the Bible in his Pittsburgh campaign before it had ever been released for examination. This translation was produced by liberal scholars under the auspices of the National Council of Churches. Additional doubts began to arise when reports of Graham's campaigns in Japan began to reach this country. Prominent on the lists of cooperating pastors and religious leaders were members of the "Kyodan," the Japanese equivalent of the liberal National Council of Churches. Noted Japanese liberals appeared on the platform with Graham. These actions caused great confusion among the missionaries in that country who had taken a stand against the "Kyodan."

Similar trends began to emerge in some of the Graham campaigns in Great Britain. Liberal churchmen participated in the crusades. Converts were advised to return to Church of England congregations that were liberal. Fundamentalist leaders in that country were chagrined, feeling that one who claimed to be a fellow fundamentalist had undercut their position. During his Scotland campaign, Billy repudiated the title "fundamentalist," declaring there was an aura of bigotry and narrowness associated with the term which he himself did not claim. In a letter to Tom Malone defending his developing policy of cooperating with liberals, Graham claimed that the doctrinal differences were not that serious. "They differ with us on the inspiration of the Bible and on the theories of the atonement."[5] Of course, the differences were much more numerous than these, but even if limited to these, they would be very significant.

It was becoming increasingly apparent that Billy Graham had shifted his position and was no longer the outspoken fundamentalist that he had once been. In writing to Dr. James, editor of a Southern Baptist paper, *Baptist Standard,* Graham remarked that he thought the Southern Baptist Cooperative Program was the finest way in the world to encourage Christians to give, and that those who opposed the program did not understand the parable of the wheat and the tares and were trying to root out the tares now rather than leave them until the judgment day. Such an endorsement was a great disappointment to many who had been opposing the Cooperative Program because it funded liberal colleges, seminaries, and missionary endeavors that were destroying the faith of thousands. Out-and-out liberals and neo-orthodox lecturers such as Emil Brunner and Robert McCracken were honored guest lecturers at Southern Baptist institutions funded by the Cooperative Program. After reading Graham's statement, John R. Rice wrote asking him, as a member of the Cooperating Board of *The Sword of the Lord,* if he could in good conscience continue to sign the doctrinal statement which appeared on the front page of every issue. It read: "An Independent Christian Weekly, Standing for the Verbal Inspiration of the Bible, the Deity of Christ, His Blood Atonement, Salvation by Faith, New Testament Soul-Winning, and the Premillennial Return of Christ. Opposes Modernism, Worldliness and Formalism." Graham, in replying, stated that he did not believe he could any longer agree to the doctrinal statement as carried by the paper and submitted his resignation from the Cooperating Board.

What happened to Billy Graham? Did he succumb to the lure of popularity? Did he come to the conclusion that to be a fundamentalist would ostracize him from most of this world's religious elite? During his 1949 campaign in Los Angeles, prior to his open break with fundamentalism, he attracted the attention of William Randolph Hearst, the newspaper magnate. In telling of his experience at Los Angeles, Graham said that one night he noticed "reporters and cameramen crawling all over the place. One of them told me they had had a memo from Mr. Hearst which said, 'Puff Graham,' and the two Hearst papers gave me great publicity. The others soon followed."[6]

That Graham has changed cannot be challenged. Whether the change is for the good or the bad is vigorously debated. Martin

Marty, a liberal, sees Graham's change as positive: "He has changed and grown. . . . All to say that Graham brought neo-evangelicalism, now evangelicalism, into an ecumenical orbit without having it lose its soul. . . . While many fundamentalists and evangelicals kept huddled in sectarian pride, Graham would refuse to come to your town unless there was broad 'church federation' backing."[7] Others feel that Graham left the high plane for the low. "But Graham is more evangelical prodigal than pilgrim. His journey has been a progressive flight from his solid fundamental Christian roots to the far country of ecumenical compromise."[8]

Bob Shuler, a fundamentalist leader who knew Graham about as well as anyone, made this observation: "But believe me, there is a great gulf between the Billy Graham I saw and knew and loved and trusted in the Los Angeles revival, as he stood without a thread of compromise and declared that he would not associate either in his personal testimony or his gospel ministry with the liberals and modernists of that great city—I say, there is an impassable barrier between that position of separation and the attitude of this great evangelist in New York and San Francisco."[9]

How sad to have to pen such words!

A Lengthy Trail of Compromise

Worms in the Big Apple

Although Billy Graham began weakening his position prior to 1957, it was in that year that the major turning point in his career was reached. In 1951 a group of fundamentalist ministers in New York City had a meeting and decided to invite the evangelist for a campaign. Graham replied to them that he would not come unless every Protestant church in the area was invited to participate and unless every cooperating church had representatives on the various campaign committees. Jack Wyrtzen, noted New York youth leader, and about ten other fundamentalists felt that they could not enter into such a campaign unless cooperating men and churches agreed to sign a fundamentalist doctrinal statement. A doctrinal statement was drawn up, approved by Graham, but rejected by certain members of the Executive Committee. A number of members resigned. Graham then wrote a letter to the Committee in which he insisted that "the committee unanimously endorse the program of an ecumenical spirit to be exhibited throughout the campaign" and should "present an ecumenical spirit of love toward those of all stripes."[10] After further discussion Graham rejected the invitation of the fundamentalists as he did another invitation issued in 1954. He did finally accept an invitation from the Protestant Council of New York, an affiliate of the National Council of Churches.

In 1957 the crusade was held in New York City. Blatant liberals were prominent, including Henry P. Van Dusen, at that time president of Union Theological Seminary in New York, one of the rankest of liberal and left-wing schools in America. In spite of this fact, Graham hailed him as a great religious leader and a convert of Billy Sunday.[11] Also included was Methodist modernist Ralph Sockman, a former member of the Communist-front organization the "Methodist Federation for Social Action." Another leading light in the crusade was John Sutherland Bonnell, pastor of the liberal Fifth Avenue Presbyterian Church. Graham was guest speaker at the left-wing Colgate-Rochester Divinity School, a bastion of apostasy. Attorney James Bennett, a long-time resident of New York City and strong Christian leader there for years, estimated that the General Crusade Committee was composed of about 120 modernists and unbelievers and about twenty fundamentalists. The Executive Committee contained about fifteen modernists and five fundamentalists.

The participation of outright liberals in a great campaign such as this was a first in American evangelism. They were prominent on the platform and many of them offered prayer at different sessions of the crusade. Their churches received hundreds of decision cards. Marble Collegiate Church, pastored by Norman Vincent Peale, whom few would claim to be a fundamentalist or Bible-preaching minister, received the most decision cards of any New York church.[12]

Bad Winds by the Golden Gate

The next crusade in San Francisco continued the trend established in New York. Members of the General Crusade Committee were such persons as Lowell Berry, a member of the trustee board of Pacific School of Religion, where at that time a practicing Jew was a member of the faculty; Fred Parr, a member of the board of the same institution; and Mrs. William Lister Rogers, originator of the infamous "Festival of Faith" held in the Cow Palace in 1955 with participants from six faiths—Christian, Jewish, Muslim, Buddhist, Hindu, and Confucian. At the opening banquet for the crusade, Graham was introduced by Sandford Fleming, former president of the Northern California Council of Churches, and for years president of the Berkeley Baptist Divinity School, an institution famous for its opposition to biblical truth.

A Continuing Downward Spiral

In 1961 Graham offered his opinion on the subject of infant baptism. In a Lutheran publication the following comments from Graham appeared: "I still have some personal problems in this matter of infant baptism, but, all of my children, with the exception of the youngest, were baptized as infants . . . I do believe that something happens at the baptism of an infant. We cannot fully understand the mysteries of God, but I believe a miracle can happen in these children so that they are regenerated, that is, made Christian, through infant baptism."[13]

At the tenth annual convention of the Full Gospel Businessmen's Fellowship in Seattle in 1962, Graham was a featured speaker. He has continued to widen his fellowship with Pentecostals and charismatics through the years. In that same year he held an ecumenical crusade in Chicago. Strong Bible-believing pastors and churches in that area opposed the crusade, but Graham went ahead full steam. Among the leaders were Charles Crowe, pastor of First Methodist Church of Wilmette, a liberal; August Hintz, a liberal Baptist and pastor of the North Shore Baptist Church; and H. S. Chandler, executive vice president of the Church Federation of Greater Chicago. Alan Redpath, then pastor of the Moody Church, addressed the pastor's breakfast and supported the crusade.

The left-wing liberal Methodist bishop, Gerald Kennedy, was chairman of Graham's Los Angeles crusade in 1963. This is the Kennedy who wrote, "I believe the testimony of the New Testament, taken as a whole, is against the doctrine of the deity of Jesus although I think it bears overwhelming witness to the divinity of Jesus."[14] Such a man hardly seems qualified to be involved in an evangelistic campaign.

In that same year Graham, in his crusade in Uruguay, featured the pastor of the First Methodist Church of Montevideo as the vice president of the campaign. This man had openly espoused evolutionary views and was reported as saying that the god of the Buddhists was the same as our God, though we approach Him differently.[15]

As he moved along in his ecumenical pathway, Graham moved closer and closer to both the National Council of Churches and the Roman Catholic church. He was the featured speaker at the National Council meeting in Miami, Florida, December 4-9, 1966. In his remarks he stated, "I am honored and privileged to be here to participate with you . . . in finding answers to some of the great problems that are faced in the field of evangelism today."[16] Just what great insights into evangelistic strategy would be provided by men who themselves were not even born again is truly an unsolved mystery. It was only a couple of years later that Graham was honored with the degree of Doctor of Humane Letters from Belmont Abbey College in Belmont, North Carolina, a Roman Catholic school. The evangelist had found bedfellows in the camps of both liberal Protestantism and apostate Roman Catholicism.

The United States Congress on Evangelism met in Minneapolis, Minnesota, the site of Graham's headquarters, September 8-13, 1969. Ninety-two denominations were represented. Two Roman Catholics appeared on the program. Ralph Abernathy, president of the Southern Christian Leadership Conference, and Leighton Ford, noted evangelist, both talked about the need for Christians to be "revolutionaries." The music of the conference featured folk singers and "Christian rock" groups. Pat Boone and the Spurrlows sang as well. Abernathy challenged his hearers to be evangelists, to eradicate war, racism, and poverty. He called upon his hearers to urge the president to "put an end to this senseless Vietnam war; to call for admission of Red China into the United Nations; . . . to demand a more equal distribution of the wealth in a society where 90 percent of the wealth is controlled by 10 percent of the nation."[17] What an evangelistic message this is! But Abernathy was not done. He declared, "We are all sons and daughters of the most high Lord—we are all brothers. . . . Take the gospel of Jesus Christ into the alleys and byways. Tell all of God's children, 'You are somebody; you are all worth something; you are God's children.' "[18] If everyone is already a child of God, why have a Congress on Evangelism?

The *New York Times* applauded the new spirit of openness among fundamentalists who were now emerging from the isolation of many years. "Conservative leaders said that this emergence from the isolation of the past has been spurred by the success of Dr. Graham. . . . It is a 'new evangelical ecumenism.' "[19]

A considerable emphasis upon the Christian's obligation to be involved in social action was evident in the Minneapolis gathering. Harold Ockenga addressed the Congress and observed, "I think we evangelicals for a period, in a reaction against the social gospel of Walter Rauschenbusch, etc., reacted a little bit too far to the right of this and made ours a circle which was self-containing. And that struggle has lasted for several decades. But some time ago, there was a enunciation of what was called the New Evangelicalism."[20] He went on to state that the New Evangelicalism restored balance to the message of the church, combining the note of personal salvation with the responsibility of social action. As is true with most of the persons who advance such contentions, he gave no scriptural authority for them. Where in the New Testament is there a command to the organized churches of Christ to engage in social reform? We fail to find any such command. It is an invention of the human mind rather than a declaration of the Almighty God.

The Disease Spreads Overseas

Attention has already been drawn to the International Congress on World Evangelization held in Lausanne, Switzerland, in 1974. Roman Catholic participants were prominent, including Benjamin Tonna, the Coordinator of Evangelism for the Vatican. The Lausanne Covenant which emerged from that gathering was doctrinally weak; part of the reason is that the Congress thought matters such as baptismal regeneration and speaking in tongues too controversial to address.

The crusade in Manila, Philippines, in 1977 was sponsored in part by the National Council of Churches of the Philippines. Graham also commented that "we have received marvellous support from the Catholic Church."[21] In that same year Graham held a crusade in Budapest, Hungary, a Communist country, where Graham lauded the religious freedom he found. No word was spoken of the believers who were suffering under the iron fist of communism. The leaders of the campaign were compromising ecumenicalists who worked hand-in-glove with the Communist regime. At least one was a member of the Executive Committee of the World Council of Churches.

Graham has helped to give credibility to the growing charismatic movement world-wide. In one interview he was asked to evaluate the charismatic movement. He declared that "it has made a great impact on virtually all denominations. It also has brought together in a new way many Christians from various backgrounds and persuasions. . . . By and large, it has been a positive force in the lives of many people."[22]

The year 1984 saw the Graham team in Great Britain in an effort called "Mission England." This campaign contained the usual mishmash of assorted religious figures. Bishop Hugh Montefiore, bishop of Birmingham, supported the Graham crusade, writing and speaking glowingly of its leader. This is none other than the same bishop who the year previous had expressed the view that persons could be saved apart from Christianity. He also declared that Jews could be saved without Christ and would not go to hell.[23] A goodly number of the supporters were connected with the Church of England, which believes, among other things, in the baptismal regeneration of infants. Liberal religious leaders such as Archbishop Robert Runcie and Bishop John Baker commended the evangelist and his work. Yes, large numbers "came forward," but to what did they come? Maurice Rowlandson, who had worked with Graham many times in England, offered this insight, "You might be surprised to see the lightheartedness of those who walk forward. They have no background; they know virtually nothing about the gospel. In fact, some of them simply want to touch the football turf."[24]

In 1985 Billy returned again to the scene of his early evangelistic ministry—Los Angeles. His crusade there was sponsored by more than two thousand churches. Robert Schuller of Crystal Cathedral fame, was one. Charles Swindoll of the First Evangelical Free Church in Fullerton was another.

The compromising method of evangelism espoused by Billy Graham has been spread to the ends of the earth through various conferences which have been sponsored in whole or in part by the Graham organization. For instance, in July 1986, eight thousand evangelists and Christian workers met in Amsterdam in what was billed as the International Conference for Itinerant Evangelists. Many of the participants came at the expense of the Graham organization. Most of the denominations were represented including Roman Catholics and members of the Orthodox churches. "At a news conference, Graham said that despite disagreements about methods or aspects of the message, evangelism is about the only word we can unite on. Agreeing on the need to spread the gospel, he said, means an 'ecumenicity' that you cannot get under any other umbrella. He also recalled his own attendance at most assemblies of the World Council of Churches, and estimated that a 'majority' of participants have come from WCC denominations."[25]

There is a great fallacy here. The promotion of evangelism does not give one the right to disobey the clear commands of Scripture. "Have no fellowship with the unfruitful works of darkness, but rather reprove them" (Eph. 5:11). We are commanded to "turn away" from those who propagate false doctrine (II Tim. 3:5). Many of the leaders and participants in Billy Graham crusades are producing "works of darkness." They are "false apostles, deceitful workers, transforming themselves into the apostles of Christ" (II Cor. 11:13). They are to be rebuked and shunned, not lauded and embraced.

Skirting the Issues in Russia

Prior to the collapse of communism in the Soviet Union, Billy Graham spoke in that country on several occasions. His actions and words displayed an alarming lack of understanding for the true situation in that land. As an example, in his 1982 visit Graham warmly embraced Metropolitan Filaret of Minsk, head of the international department of the state-controlled Russian Orthodox church. Remember that such persons were in power by the permission of Communist authorities and were obligated to cooperate fully with their atheistic leaders. While he was preaching in the Moscow Baptist Church, a young woman unfurled a banner which read, "We have more than 150 prisoners for the work of the gospel." Graham ignored it. When asked about it later he said that even in the United States people are arrested for causing disturbances. Commenting further, he declared, "There are many differences in religion here and in the way it is practiced in the United States. But that does not mean there is no religious freedom in the Soviet Union."[26] At the moment he was speaking those words, hundreds of courageous Christians were in Soviet concentration camps because of their loyalty to Jesus Christ and the gospel. This writer has fellowshiped with many of them since the fall of communism. What a blow it was to them to hear reports that the world's leading evangelist declared that there was religious freedom in Russia! We must give *Time* magazine, no bastion of fundamentalism, credit for its insightful remarks:

> Yet, throughout the week, Graham seemed oblivious to the precarious role of religion in a country that endorses scientific atheism and outlaws public evangelism. It is a country where only the officially-sanctioned Russian Orthodox church is permitted to exist in relative peace, where Protestant groups are tolerated only if they accept government restrictions and are harassed if they do not. The Baptists who heard Graham's gospel can hold worship services, but they cannot preach the Word of God in public or bring up their children with religious instruction.[27]

The Baptists here described, by the way, were of the "registered churches," those who had agreed to obey the demands of their Communist overlords. They were restricted, but their more courageous brethren, the "unregistered churches" were even more restricted. They were not allowed to own church buildings, had to meet in secret places, and were stripped of their finest leaders, who were packed off to concentration camps.

As a supposedly mature Christian leader, Graham should have demonstrated far more discernment and courage than was evident. Again, for the sake of so-called open doors, he compromised. M. Stanton Evans was correct when he stated that "Graham's trip was a mindless, stunning propaganda triumph for the Soviets."[28]

A few years later the evangelist was invited to take part in marking a thousand years of "Christianity" in the Soviet Union (assuming one can call the formalistic, liturgical Orthodox church a part of Christianity). The Russian church traces its roots back to 988 when Prince Vladmir had the people of Kievan Rus (later called Russia) baptized in the Dnieper River near Kiev. Graham's participation included preaching in Orthodox cathedrals. Of course he said nothing to contradict the false teaching of that ancient church. He declared rather, "I am deeply honored to join with you at this historic and joyous occasion commemorating the 1,000th anniversary of the baptism of Russia, occasioned by the baptism of Kievan

Prince Vladmir." He also remarked, "This occasion of the millennium of the baptism of Russia reminds all of us who are believers in Christ that the things which unite us are far more important than the things which tend to isolate us."[29]

> It was an improbable scenario: an American clergyman preaching an evangelistic sermon in the Soviet Union amid the trappings of a staid Russian Orthodox Cathedral, a bearded prelate in golden robes and mitre standing approvingly at his side; and Soviet government officials, and liberal Protestant leaders of the World Council of Churches sprinkled among the thousands fortunate enough to be shoehorned inside. It happened during last month's millennial celebration of the Russian Orthodox Church. . . . The event, featuring evangelist Billy Graham at Saint Vladmir Cathedral in Kiev, capsulized some of the dramatic changes apparently taking place . . . in the church.[30]

Not one word of denunciation for the apostate practices of the host church! No Jeremiah-like rebukes of the obvious departure from the Word of God. No courageous exposure of the "scribes and Pharisees, hypocrites," such as came from the lips of our Lord (e.g., Matt. 23:13-14). There were "positive" statements, innocuous utterances that would soothe and not convict.

When asked what kind of religious freedoms the Soviet citizens had, Graham replied, "Some groups get extremely fanatical and they do things they think are right when actually they are breaking Soviet law and they get into trouble. But you can go to church. They're building seven new Baptist churches in Moscow."[31] What Graham failed to say was that these churches were being built only by those compromising Baptists who succumbed to Communist pressure and cooperated with the pagan government. Baptists who refused to compromise their convictions were mercilessly hounded, imprisoned, and killed. When the early apostles were threatened by religious and political authorities and told that they could not preach the gospel, they replied, "We ought to obey God rather than men" (Acts 5:29). There is a higher law than Soviet law (or that of any other government). It is the law of God, and it is to that law we must adhere even when to do so brings us in conflict with governmental authorities.

Tainting the Waters

The compromises of Billy Graham have had a widespread and devastating impact. His fingerprints are very evident upon the New Evangelical movement. The principles he has espoused throughout most of his ministry are now accepted by large numbers of evangelicals.

The Broad Way

The spirit of openness and broadness now seen in so much of evangelicalism was initially fostered by Graham. It was he who began reaching out to the liberals years ago when many Bible-believers opposed it. In explaining his broader position, he seems to suggest that he is exempt from the biblical standards which others follow. "My position as a 'proclaimer of the gospel' is entirely different than if I were the president of a Bible school or the pastor of a church or a professor of theology. While holding a firm theological position, yet in the proclamation of the gospel there is flexibility of fellowship."[32] But does God allow a wider scope of fellowship for an evangelist than he does for other believers? Where is this principle found in Scripture? Can he fellowship with the National Council of Churches crowd while faithful pastors, seeking to maintain the purity of their churches, refuse to do so? Does God have a double standard?

Already we have seen that this evangelist is loathe to condemn false religious systems and their teachers. Never does he expose the apostasy of such groups as the National and World Council of Churches. Scripture, however, exhorts faithful ministers of God to openly combat teachers of error, and to "rebuke them sharply" (Titus 1:13). Paul was bold to identify by name Hymenaeus and Alexander, who had made shipwreck of the faith (I Tim. 1:20). Even the "apostle of love," John, identified the proud braggart, Diotrophes, and condemned his actions (III John 9). There is no special virtue in just being "positive." There are negative aspects of truth as well, and these must also be presented.

Through the efforts of Billy Graham, many feel that religious liberalism is no longer the monstrous foe that our forefathers thought it to be. The early fundamentalists waged battle against modernism (liberalism) and gave no quarter. Today we are told that these liberals really are not so bad. From where did this idea arise among those who claim to follow the Bible? It arose from Billy Graham's crusades, where liberals and fundamentalists mixed readily. "The professing Church can no longer be divided into two camps: modernism . . . and fundamentalism. . . . For the gigantic evangelistic impact spearheaded by Billy Graham has broken this division down, and has engendered new reactions."[33] Younger pastors and Christian leaders, holding Graham up as a model, have little fear to broaden their fellowship. David Fisher, pastor of the Crystal Free Church in a suburb of Minneapolis, said, "We're living out the dream of Billy Graham, and others who modeled the kind of thing we do. They lowered the barriers and reached out."[34] The same article declares, "In many ways the changing mood is a tribute to the ecumenical efforts of evangelist Billy Graham, who decided more than 30 years ago never to do a crusade in a city without the agreement of the local clergy."[35]

Without a doubt Graham has done much to build the ecumenical church and to give it prestige.

> One often-cited example of effective "local ecumenism" is the crusade-style ministry of Billy Graham. Since the 1950s, the Baptist evangelist's frequent crusades have brought together local clergy from various denominations—some with little experience or interest in traditional ecumenism—who begin working weeks in advance to promote the event. Though Graham may not intend to be, observes Richard Mouw, provost at Fuller Theological Seminary in Pasadena, California, he is "probably the most important ecumenical figure alive."[36]

William Ward Ayer, famous radio preacher and long-time pastor of the large Calvary Baptist Church of New York City, long ago observed that Graham's ecumenical evangelism was aiding the ecumenical movement.

> It is sad to see many of our brilliant minds so deeply deceived by the enemy. Liberalism has changed its nomenclature but not its nature, and some of our enthusiastic and blithesome theologians feel they can bridge the chasm between redemptive Christianity and non-redemptive religion by friendly and amiable cooperation. But the chasm is unbridgeable—it is a "great gulf fixed." The flimsy structure this group is building will prove a trap for millions who attempt the crossing; for on one side is the Church, the Bride of Christ, and on the other, the "Coming Great

Church" of your editorial, which . . . in reality is the harlot church, and these two can never be joined.[37]

Bravo for William Ward Ayer! Would there were more courageous servants like him today.

Put aside "peripheral" doctrinal differences—this is the message sent by Graham to impressionable young leaders of the church. For this reason he tries to walk the middle line on difficult and disputed doctrines. Even his friend, Carl Henry, observed, "His books tend to gloss over doctrinal divisions within evangelical circles."[38] The truth is, Billy Graham wants everyone for his friend. He does not wish to offend the liberal, the charismatic, or the Catholic. He wants to be on all sides of a question at the same time. But the prophet of God cannot take such a stance. When God gave Jeremiah his commission, He told him he was to "root out, and to pull down, and to destroy, and to throw down, to build, and to plant" (Jer. 1:10). Here were four negatives and two positives. Error must be demolished and thorn-covered ground cleared before progress can be made on a building of truth. Destruction of the wrong must precede the erection of the right. One cannot say, as Graham did, when asked for his appraisal of the charismatic movement, "I think the charismatic movement has been used of God in many areas of the world, for example, Sweden."[39] How can one say that a movement which is theologically in error is being greatly used of God? Does God employ erroneous theology to achieve His purposes?

Holding Hands with the Pope

Graham's close relationship with the Roman Catholic church has indeed been a puzzle to many. The Roman church teaches salvation by baptism, the necessity of good works to earn heaven, the repetition of Christ's sacrifice upon the altars of the church, the impossibility of knowing that one is going to heaven, the necessity of venerating the virgin Mary, and countless other heresies. In spite of this, Graham, when ministering in Poland, preached in Roman Catholic churches and was received warmly by their leaders. One Roman Catholic leader hailed Graham as typical of evangelicals with whom the Catholic church can have "fruitful dialogue."[40] The executive vice president of Belmont Abbey College, a Roman Catholic school that bestowed an honorary doctorate upon Billy Graham, gave his opinion of the evangelist's ministry: "Knowing

65

the tremendous influence of Billy Graham among Protestants, and now the realization and acknowledgment among Catholics of his devout and sincere appeal to the teachings of Christ which he alone preaches, I would state that he could bring Catholics and Protestants together in a healthy ecumenical spirit. . . . Billy Graham is preaching a moral and evangelical theology most acceptable to Catholics."[41]

One would think that an evangelist, one specializing in the "evangel," the gospel, would call men away from worthless idols and systems of error into the light of New Testament truth. An evangelist is to point lost and groping men to the clear way of salvation. This way of salvation is not found within the Roman Catholic church. Yet the evangelist continues to populate Catholic churches with his converts.

> A confused Romanist [in the 1960s] wrote to Dr. Graham expressing his concern over the fact that "many of the old confidences are being shaken," and he asked the evangelist: "Where will it all stop?" Dr. Graham replied to him through the "Billy Graham Answers" column of the *Chattanooga Free Press,* and said, "Your church is going through turbulence which both lay and clergy forces are bringing about. . . .
>
> "Practices of worship may change, but the sincerity of our devotion need not be altered. . . .
>
> "Above all don't pull out of the church! Stay in, stay close to the Lord, and use these experiences as an opportunity to help your church be what God intends and what the world needs."[42]

Upon what scriptural ground can a gospel evangelist tell a believer in Christ to remain in an apostate church that denies the very truths he is trying to preach? How tragic! How heart-rending that a man who should know better would give such advice as this! "Woe unto them that call evil good, and good evil; that put darkness for light, and light for darkness; that put bitter for sweet, and sweet for bitter" (Isa. 5:20). If one who is seeking to lead men and women into the light cannot distinguish the light from the darkness, how confused his leadership will be!

Hear the testimony of one who took the advice of the evangelist to his own spiritual detriment. He was saved in the Graham crusade in New York City. He told the counselor who dealt with him that he belonged to the Roman Catholic church. Only fourteen years old at the time, he listened intently to Dr. Graham as he gave instructions to those who had come forward at the conclusion of the service. They were told to go back to the church from which they had come. "Since Billy Graham sent me to the Catholic Church I was under the impression that this was the right church. . . . What did I gain from the Billy Graham Crusade? I gained about one year and a half in darkness and ignorance of the Bible because Billy Graham sent me to the Catholic Church."[43]

Opening Arms to the Liberals

The policy of referring converts to liberal churches was defended by W. R. White who was then President of Baylor University in Texas. He declared it to be a healthy practice because "new converts with a genuine experience of grace are planted in those liberal churches as a New Testament witness. . . . Furthermore, Christ, Paul, and all the great evangelists followed a similar pattern."[44] To read such a false statement as this from a Christian leader is breathtaking. How could a Baptist preacher, professing to believe in the Baptist distinctive of regenerate church membership, ever for one moment defend the practice of sending converts to churches that do not practice regenerate church membership? One does not join a church in order to evangelize its members. One joins a church in order to worship God with other true believers, to be taught the correct doctrines of Scripture, and then to go forth to evangelize the lost.

Time has taken its toll. In the early days of Graham's compromises, there was considerable opposition among fundamentalists and even those who had been his closest friends. Now, however, vocal and public opposition to him has decreased to a mere murmur. Even those who state that they do not agree with him nevertheless tend to keep silent on the issue for fear of disturbing their congregations or being thought of as "fighting fundamentalists." "They have healed also the hurt of the daughter of my people slightly, saying, Peace, peace; when there is no peace" (Jer. 6:14). But peace cannot be purchased at the price of the compromise of truth. It is too high a price to pay.

The question naturally arises: "If Graham is not a liberal himself, why do liberals support his crusades?" One obvious reason is the fact that Graham does not denounce liberalism as most of the old-time evangelists did. He steadfastly refuses to expose the errors of the apostates but rather applauds them and honors them as worthy spiritual guides. Possibly one of the most succinct answers to our question was given by a leading British liberal, Leslie Weatherhead, who was at the time pastor of City Temple in London, England.

> I do not personally agree with some of Billy Graham's theology ... but I certainly accept the value of Billy Graham's witness and I note two things about him. He does not thrust his theological views on another person, and secondly, though in all denominations Ministers have published criticisms of him, he has never once, to my knowledge, lifted his voice or pen to tell us that in his nostrils our theology stinks. . . . I should have thought that any Minister who preaches to small congregations might rejoice that Billy Graham is helping to fill our churches for us. We can teach people theology when we have got somebody to teach.[45]

In essence he is saying, "Billy Graham can get people into my church with his evangelical theology, and then I will proceed to teach them my liberal theology." A great tradeoff, is it not? Liberal theology is so bereft of power it cannot fill churches; so it will feed off of the evangelical theology that does fill churches.

This same spirit of compromise initiated and promoted by Billy Graham now is pervasive among evangelical churches everywhere. Do whatever you must do to get crowds, to fill the churches. It is religious pragmatism run amuck. It is the "theology of the convenient."

Scriptural Principles Versus Ecumenical Evangelism

There are several principles of Scripture which serve to sit in judgment on the operational philosophy of ecumenical evangelism.

1. We are not to fellowship with liberals in order to win them to Christ.

By "fellowshiping" with liberals is meant a cooperation with them in a religious context for the purposes of achieving spiritual results. "Put your warm arm of love around the liberal and perhaps he will change." This is the approach of many. It is not, however, the approach of God. God is first and foremost concerned about the purity of the church. His holiness and the holiness of His people must be preserved at all costs. God is more concerned about holiness than He is about results. God is not interested in successful evangelism which jeopardizes the holy character of the church. "Be ye holy; for I am holy" (I Pet. 1:16). Holiness involves separation from all that is evil. Religious liberalism is evil; therefore, holiness involves separation from it. After describing the awful moral and spiritual degeneration of the last days, especially noting the popularity of hypocritical religion, Paul instructs the believer to "turn away" from such (II Tim. 3:5). The Graham philosophy denies that we should "turn away" (refuse them fellowship) but offers a "better" plan—join with them in religious endeavors.

The Graham philosophy on this point was set many years ago when he wrote a definitive article entitled "Fellowship and Separation." He said, "There can be no escaping the conclusion that the main stress of the New Testament is upon fellowship rather than upon separation. The call is not so much to come out as to come together."[46]

Let us analyze this succinct statement of Graham's approach to this critical matter. It is true that the New Testament has a great deal to say about fellowship. But *it is fellowship among born-again believers,* not fellowship among believers and unbelievers. Many of the religious leaders with whom Graham fellowships are rank unbelievers. They reject many of the cardinal doctrines of the Bible. Despite their claims to be Christians, they are not Christians in the biblical sense of that term. But Graham persists in perpetuating the myth that they are Christians who simply have different views on some matters. It is also true that the New Testament teaches both fellowship and separation. The total number of verses on fellowship may be greater in number (I have not counted them) because the epistles of the New Testament were written to be used in the assemblies of God's people where that emphasis is needed. There is no lack of clear teaching, however, on the subject of separation from that which is evil. God, as always, has the proper balance in His Word.

2. We are not to honor false prophets as true Christian leaders.

Illustrations have already been given of Graham's accolades for apostate church leaders. Graham was an honored guest at the installation of James Albert Pike as the Bishop Coadjutor of California for the Protestant Episcopal Church of the U.S.A. Pike was an unbeliever of the first magnitude, an open opponent of precious biblical truths. When Billy first began to push his ecumenical agenda in the 1957 New York crusade, he wrote a letter in which he denied the truth of the criticisms that were being leveled at the crusade, and said, "The sponsoring committee are godly men who are seeking to reach New York's vast population with the testimony of the risen Christ."[47] What kind of men were these "godly men" who served? One of them was James Sutherland Bonnell, a leading liberal. Attorney James Bennett, who courageously opposed Graham's New York crusade and lost many friends because of his stand, wrote:

> To add more to the confusion, a friend of mine, who telephoned the New York headquarters of the Billy Graham Crusade, was told that they did not classify Dr. John Sutherland Bonnell as a modernist. My friend was surprised because he knew personally that Dr. Bonnell had refused in 1951 to sign a fundamental statement of faith submitted to him by the Billy Graham organization in existence at that time, and on March 23, 1954, he wrote an article published in *Look* magazine, implying very plainly that he did not believe several of the fundamental Gospel doctrines, including the Bodily Resurrection of Jesus.[48]

How can men promote the "testimony of a risen Christ" when they do not even believe in a "risen Christ"?

How did Paul handle false prophets who denied the faith? He warned against those who "resist the truth," and called them "men of corrupt minds, reprobate concerning the faith" (II Tim. 3:8). Never would Paul have considered placing such men in positions of leadership in an evangelistic campaign. They themselves needed to be evangelized and should not be in charge of evangelizing others. They are lost souls in desperate need of a Savior. Nor was the Old Testament prophet Jeremiah flattering to the false prophets of the day: "Woe be unto the pastors that destroy and scatter the sheep of my pasture! saith the Lord. . . . I will visit upon you the evil of your doings" (Jer. 23:1-2). Billy Graham does not make pronouncements like that. For this reason he is popular among the false prophets of the day.

3. We are not to disobey the Scriptures in order to win souls for Christ.

Much modern evangelism seems based upon the premise that God needs all the help He can get in getting people saved; so if we must "fudge" a bit regarding scriptural principles, we are certainly justified in doing so. The end (the salvation of souls) justifies the means (cooperating with unbelievers). Where in Scripture is this principle taught?

I remember years ago when a distinguished pastor, William Ashbrook, and I were called to the West Coast to address gatherings of pastors on the issue of Billy Graham's ecumenical crusades. My friend arose to give his message. His first words were: "The primary business of a Christian is not to win souls." There were gasps and grunts. He waited a few moments before uttering his second sentence. "The primary business of a Christian is to do the will of God." This is true. We are not saying, of course, that Christians ought not to win souls. They must do it, however, within the context of scriptural principles. When Peter and his friends had toiled all the night and failed to catch any fish, the Master Fisherman took charge. Peter, no slouch as a fisherman himself, recognized that a Greater was in the boat, and said, "Master . . . at thy word I will let down the net" (Luke 5:5). In other words, "In accordance with your will, I will do my fishing." Many fish were caught, and Christ informed them that in the future they would "catch men" and not fish. To catch men requires as much obedience to the Word of Christ as did the task of catching fish. We must do our spiritual fishing in obedience to the revealed principles of Christ. Here is where ecumenical evangelism fails.

Saul learned a hard lesson: You cannot substitute a good thing for the best thing—total obedience to God. The first king of Israel was specifically commanded by God to smite the Amalekites, the heathen enemies of God and His people, and to destroy them and all that they had (I Sam. 15:2-3). Ignoring that command and taking matters into his own hands, Saul spared a portion of the flocks and herds of the Amalekites. When Samuel the prophet reappeared, he enquired whether Saul had completely obeyed the Lord. He discovered that he had not. Saul, however, had a ready defense of his disobedience. He had disobeyed God's instructions about the animals of Amalek so that he could obey God's instructions about the required sacrifices. The animals he had spared were to be used as sacrifices to God. At that point Samuel uttered a monumental statement: "Hath the Lord as great delight in burnt offerings and sacrifices, as in obeying the voice of the Lord? Behold, to obey is better than sacrifice, and to hearken than the fat of rams. For rebellion is as the sin of witchcraft, and stubbornness is as iniquity and idolatry" (I Sam 15:22-23).

Billy Graham and his followers have justified their disobedience to God's prohibitions of cooperation with the apostates with the plea that they are winning souls to Christ and that this overshadows all other considerations. This line of reasoning, however, is obviously contrary to the principle given by Samuel. Sacrifices were good, proper, and scriptural when practiced in accordance with the will of God. When practiced apart from the will of God, they were not acceptable. So it is with evangelism. Evangelism is commanded in Scripture, but so is obedience to God. We cannot evangelize while disobeying God.

4. We are not to disobey the Scriptures on the plea that we are displaying God's love.

Many Christians have a distorted view of the nature of God's love. New Evangelicals have stated, "The badge of Christian discipleship is not orthodoxy, but love." Current New Evangelicals trumpet the fact that fundamentalist separatists are harsh and abrasive while they are loving. Love, according to them, overlooks doctrinal error and embraces almost everyone who claims to be a Christian. Love does not criticize nor condemn. Love merely affirms.

It is very plain from the Scriptures that love and obedience walk together. Consider these words of our Lord.

1. "If ye love me, keep my commandments" (John 14:15).
2. "He that hath my commandments and keepeth them, he it is that loveth me" (John 14:21).
3. "If a man love me, he will keep my words" (John 14:23).

The Lord commands in His Word that His people "have no fellowship with the unfruitful works of darkness, but rather reprove them" (Eph. 5:11). Liberal preachers are sources of the "works of darkness." To fellowship with them is to disobey this command; to do so is, in fact, *un*loving.

This passage, plus the utterances of Christ just cited from John's Gospel, declare clearly that if one would obey Christ, one must refuse cooperation with apostates. The proponents of ecumenical evangelism, however, do not agree with this premise. In the face of scriptural admonitions to the contrary, they continue to cozy up to the Christ-denying church leaders.

5. *We are not to seek to please as wide a constituency as possible in order to gain a sympathetic hearing for the gospel.*

One of the points that Graham defenders have made is the fact that hundreds of people from liberal churches hear the gospel of Christ because their pastors and churches cooperate in the crusades. This is a flagrant case of religious pragmatism. We employ whatever methods work regardless of the scriptural principles involved. Certainly this was not the methodology of the early apostles and their followers. Paul, in combating the Judaizers who were trying to flavor the gospel of Christ to suit the palates of Jewish hearers, declared, "For do I now persuade men, or God? or do I seek to please men? for if I yet pleased men, I should not be the servant of Christ" (Gal 1:10). "Men-pleasers simply do not hurl *anathemas* against those who proclaim false gospels."[49] An apt observation indeed! But, regrettably, Billy Graham does not "hurl anathemas" at those great number of supporters who preach a false gospel. His failure to do so wins him many friends, but does it fulfill the commands of the Lord?

6. *We are not to condone false doctrine as though it were of little consequence.*

The Roman Catholic church teaches heresy, but Billy Graham condones and encourages its leaders. They teach many doctrines which are directly opposed to the Word of God; yet their leaders and members are featured or included in Graham crusades and conferences. So also is it with the charismatics who insist that sign-gifts are still operable today. Paul did not mince words about false doctrine when he wrote, "Now the Spirit speaketh expressly, that in the latter times some shall depart from the faith, giving heed to seducing spirits, and doctrines of devils" (I Tim. 4:1). The great apostle of love, John, was not only concerned about the manifestation of love but also about the repudiation of error. He did not advocate a naive gullibility concerning doctrine. "Beloved, believe not every spirit, but try the spirits whether they are of God: because many false prophets are gone out into the world" (I John 4:1). In pursuing that theme he said that we should be able to differentiate between the "spirit of truth, and the spirit of error" (I John 4:6).

Spiritual discernment is important and must be exercised. There is a vast difference between truth and error and this difference ought not to be ignored or glossed over.

7. *We are to recognize that sound doctrine has priority over fellowship and that true fellowship is based upon sound doctrine.*

Doctrine has fallen on evil times. Few wish to battle for what they call "peripheral" doctrines. They wish to emphasize instead our unity in Christ and the blessings they see flowing from that.

God's view of doctrine, however, is much stronger than that of some evangelicals. When the first local church was founded in Jerusalem, its characteristics were noted. There were four of them, but the first one mentioned is steadfastness in the "apostles' doctrine" (Acts 2:42). Fellowship, breaking of bread, and prayers followed the mention of doctrine. It is noteworthy that doctrine is the first on the list. It would not be of such paramount importance to many evangelicals today. A little later in apostolic history Paul was concerned that "the things which become sound doctrine," be taught in the church (Titus 2:1). Often Paul refers to "sound doctrine," that is, doctrine which is healthy and not contaminated by error. He was most concerned that this kind of doctrine be perpetuated in the churches.

Ecumenical evangelism is not in line with God's program and principles. It is an attempt to bring together that which should not be together. "Can two walk together, except they be agreed?" (Amos 3:3). "What fellowship hath righteousness with unrighteousness? and what communion hath light with darkness?" (II Cor. 6:14). God has separated light from darkness and no one, not even in the cause of evangelism, should attempt to take down those divinely erected barriers.

Notes

[1] George Marsden, *Reforming Fundamentalism*, p. 167.

[2] Doug Reed, "Billy Graham: Maturing Leader," *Asheville* (N.C.) *Citizen Times,* 19 October 1958.

[3] Personal correspondence from Billy Graham to Dr. Bob Jones, Jr., and Dr. Bob Jones, Sr., 16 January 1947 and 23 October 1950.

[4] Robert Shuler, editor, *Methodist Challenge,* October 1957.

[5] Letter from Billy Graham to Tom Malone, cited in *Sword of the Lord,* 17 May 1957, p. 11.

6."Billy Graham," *Time,* 20 March 1950, pp. 72-73.

7Martin Marty, "Reflections on Graham by a Former Grump," *Christianity Today,* 18 November 1988, pp. 24-25.

8Letter from Joseph A. Brazeal to *Greenville* (S.C.) *News,* 5 May 1986.

9Robert Shuler, editor, *The Methodist Challenge,* October 1957.

10Billy Graham, letter to Executive Committee, New York Crusade, 1951.

11News item, *U.S. News and World Report,* 27 September 1957.

12*Christian Life,* September 1957, p. 25.

13Wilfred Bockelman, "A Lutheran Looks at Billy Graham," *Lutheran Standard,* 10 October 1961.

14Gerald Kennedy, *God's Good News,* p. 125.

15News report, *Baptist Bible Tribune,* 8 March 1963.

16."Billy Graham at the NCC Assembly," *Christian Beacon,* 5 January 1967.

17Merle Hull, "U.S. Congress on Evangelism," *Baptist Bulletin,* November 1969, p. 11.

18Ibid.

19."New Liberal Mood Is Found Among Fundamentalist Protestants," *New York Times,* 14 September 1969.

20M. H. Reynolds, Jr., "The Muddy Water of Mainstream Evangelical Thought," October 1969.

21*Christianity Today,* 31 December 1977, p. 37.

22."Candid Conversation with the Evangelist." *Christianity Today,* 17 July 1981, p. 23.

23Malcom Watt, "Mission England: Is It Scriptural?" *Bible League Quarterly,* January-March 1984, p. 21.

24William Petersen, "The Mission in England," *Evangelical Newsletter,* 10 August 1984, p. 4.

25From Ecumenical Press Service, cited in *Christian Beacon,* 7 August 1986, p. 4.

26."Inside Washington," *Human Events,* 22 May 1982, pp. 5-6.

27M. Stanton Evans, "The Brainwashing of Billy Graham," *Human Events,* 5 June 1982, p. 7.

28Ibid.

29M.H. Reynolds, Jr., "Mikhail Gorbachev and Billy Graham," *Foundation,* September 1988, p. 4.

30Edward Plowman, "Graham Joins Russian Church Festivities," *Christianity Today,* 15 July 1988, p. 49.

[31]"My Role Is to Bring Peace and Understanding," *USA Today,* 15 May 1985.

[32]Open letter from Billy Graham, "Separation or Fellowship."

[33]Editorial, "Theology, Evangelism, Ecumenism," *Christianity Today,* 20 January 1958, p. 20.

[34]"New Evangelical Churches Promoting Ecumenical Spirit," *Minneapolis Star-Tribune,* 28 May 1989.

[35]Ibid.

[36]"Reuniting the Flock," *U.S. News and World Report,* 4 March 1991, p. 50.

[37]William Ward Ayer, letter to the editor, *United Evangelical Action,* 15 June 1958.

[38]Carl Henry, "Firm on the Fundamentals," *Christianity Today,* 18 November 1988, p. 19.

[39]"Taking the World's Temperature," *Christianity Today,* 13 September 1977, p. 17.

[40]John Sheerin, "Dialogue With Evangelicals Like Billy Graham," *The Catholic World,* June 1965, pp. 158-59.

[41]Letter to Mr. Julius Taylor from the Rev. Cuthbert E. Allen, Executive Vice President, Belmont Abbey College, Belmont, North Carolina.

[42]Watt, p. 36.

[43]Testimony by Jaffet Perez, published in *Baptist Examiner,* 16 May 1964, p. 1.

[44]W. R. White, "Modern Pharisees and Sadducees," *Baptist Standard,* 2 July 1958, p. 5.

[45]From "City Temple Tidings," quoted in *Banner of Truth,* May-June 1966, p. 2.

[46]Billy Graham, "Fellowship and Separation," *Decision,* August 1961, p. 14.

[47]Letter by Billy Graham, published in *Herald of His Coming,* 23 November 1956, p. 8.

[48]James Bennett, "Supplementary Statement of James Bennett," 1954.

[49]Donald K. Campbell, "Galatians," *Bible Knowledge Commentary,* 2:591.

4 **R**eaping the Whirlwind

The Young and Worldly Evangelicals

Students often tend to become more radical than their teachers. This certainly can be seen in the development of the New Evangelicalism. As the movement has progressed, many younger members of it have adopted theological, ethical, and moral positions that have gone far beyond those taken by the earlier New Evangelicals and have brought concern even to them. One compromise begets another and before long some have traveled a very long way down the wrong road.

By the 1970s a more radical brand of New Evangelicalism had begun to emerge. Its progress was noted in two volumes by Richard Quebedeaux, *The Young Evangelicals* and *The Worldly Evangelicals*. The seeds sown by the earlier New Evangelical leaders began to produce a bitter harvest indeed. So far had some of these "new image" evangelicals gone that even their mentors became alarmed. The original New Evangelical philosophy has returned like a boomerang to strike the very ones who sent it forth.

Articulate and likeable persons were numbered in this group. Joe Roos came to the fore in connection with the People's Christian Coalition, a group promoting liberal political views. Leighton Ford, Billy Graham's brother-in-law, rose to prominence as an evangelist. Tom Skinner, a former Harlem gang leader, was among them. Authors such as Bruce Larson would be representative of this type of evangelical. Larson produced an "enlightened" view of sex for Christians in his book *Ask Me to Dance*. Women such as Nancy Hardesty became quite active.

Characteristics of the "Left Wing"

Young and worldly New Evangelicalism should surely be characterized as the "left wing" of this movement. The "right wing" would be composed of older New Evangelicals such as Kenneth

Kantzer, Carl Henry, and Harold Lindsell. Some of them have expressed dismay at the radical thoughts coming from the left wing, particularly in the area of biblical inspiration. When one sows to the wind, one will reap the whirlwind (Hos. 8:7).

An Increasing Mood of Antagonism Toward Fundamentalism

Back in the mid-seventies Richard Quebedeaux noted, "Most people outside the evangelical community itself . . . are totally unaware of the profound changes that have occurred within evangelicalism during the last several years."[1] Another author went a bit further when he warned, "What evangelicals need to realize is that there is a creeping latitudinarianism in their own circles, especially among the so-called young evangelicals who are understandably trying to break loose from the theological and cultural rigidity and provincialism of their backgrounds."[2]

One could add that it has ceased "creeping" and is now running. There are New Evangelical churches who boast about "repatriating fundamentalists." All manner of wild accusations are raised against fundamentalists who, according to these prophets of gloom, have saddled the people of God with ridiculous and impossible rules and regulations and thus stunted their growth in the Lord. A good many people are attracted to such churches because they carry chips on their shoulders against the fundamentalist churches in which they were raised.

Weakening the Word of God

By and large the original New Evangelicals were committed to the historic position of verbal, plenary inspiration. However, cracks began to appear in the foundation, even in the early days of Fuller Theological Seminary, and these cracks began to widen. Dewey Beegle in his book *The Inspiration of Scripture* said unashamedly, "We need to remind ourselves that the verbal plenary formulation of inspiration is after all, only a doctrine—a non-Biblical doctrine at that."[3] Later, a professor at Fuller Seminary, Paul King Jewett, produced a volume entitled *Man as Male and Female* in which he concluded that Paul was a victim of his culture and erred in making some of the statements he had made concerning female subordination. He declared that the Bible could still be authoritative to believers even though it contains errors such as this.

Harold Lindsell, who has impeccable credentials as one of the early New Evangelicals, produced a blockbuster with his volume *The Battle for the Bible* (1976). He clearly shows that many so-called "evangelicals" have jettisoned the doctrine of inerrancy and openly state that the Bible contains errors. His chapter on "The Strange Case of Fuller Theological Seminary" details the internal struggles of the faculty of that school over the question of biblical inspiration. (Lindsell was one of the original faculty members at Fuller.)

Fuller Seminary replied to Lindsell in a special publication entitled *The Authority of Scripture at Fuller.* The document makes clear that Fuller Seminary does not hold to the doctrine of biblical inerrancy (infallibility) *as this historically has been understood among Bible-believing Christians.* Fuller has redefined the terms— the Bible is infallible in matters of faith and practice, but contains various errors (some of them prefer the term "inconsistencies") in matters of "lesser importance." One of their writers, William LaSor, declared the Bible to be "remarkably reliable and accurate," but this is a far cry from stating that the Bible is "infallible." The same writer comments, "There is in my mind a clear difference between saying that the Bible is entirely without error in all that it teaches, and in saying that the Bible is without error in all matters (such as geology, astronomy, genealogy, figures, etc.) when these matters are not essential to the teaching of the context."[4]

In other words, the concept held by Fuller Seminary and many young and worldly evangelicals is that the Bible is infallible when it "teaches" us some doctrine or truth, but it is not necessarily infallible when it speaks of other matters such as geology or history. This statement reflects a very serious condition in the modern church. To call into question the absolute infallibility of God's holy Word is a high crime and worthy of public censure. For too long some evangelicals have tried to cover up such matters by appealing to "Christian love" or the necessity of "maintaining unity." We do not need either love or unity at the expense of truth.

One of the "old-guard" New Evangelicals, Carl Henry, raised this warning some years ago: "Yet a growing vanguard of young graduates of evangelical colleges who hold doctorates from non-evangelical divinity centers now question or disown inerrancy and the doctrine is held less consistently by evangelical faculties. . . . Some retain the term and reassure supportive constituencies but nonetheless stretch the term's meaning."[5] Another writer had a similar but more detailed observation that

> a surprising array of equally dedicated evangelicals is forming to insist that acceptance of historic Christian doctrines does not require belief in an inerrant book. This latter group maintains that where "inerrancy" refers to what the Holy Spirit is saying through Biblical writers, the word is rightly used, but to go beyond this in defining inerrancy is to suggest "a precision alien to the minds of the Bible writers and their own use of Scriptures," as one statement put it.
>
> What has made it a new ball game today is the emergence of a new type of evangelical. These persons accept the cardinal doctrines of Christianity in their full and literal meaning but agree that the higher critics have a point: there are errors in Scripture, and some of its precepts must be recognized as being culturally and historically conditioned.[6]

Plainly the young and worldly evangelicals had adopted a less strict view of the inspiration of Scripture. This was bound to have a dilatory effect upon churches and Christian institutions as time passed. One leading "young evangelical" put it this way: "This position—affirming that Scripture is inerrant and infallible in its teaching on matters of faith and conduct but not necessarily in all its assertions concerning history and the cosmos—is gradually becoming ascendant among the most highly respected evangelical theologians."[7]

It is approaching twenty years since some of these statements were written. The situation has been deteriorating steadily since that time.

Bowing at the Shrine of Science

The young and worldly evangelicals became very enamored with modern scientific thought. Many of them felt that because fundamentalists resisted so much that was taught in the name of science, they had earned the distinction of being "obscurantists." It is true that fundamentalists have opposed many modern scientific theories, but such opposition does not make them obscurantists. The preponderance of modern scientific philosophy is in deadly opposition to the revealed Word of God. Where there are valid scientific principles, we accept them. They exist because they are part of

God's design for creation. We are grateful for such advances and discoveries in the scientific world which have made our lives more pleasant. The underlying concepts, however, which are embraced by the majority of scientists today are diametrically opposed to God's Word. Interestingly, one of the founders of the New Evangelicalism, Carl Henry, recognized this and in a masterful way discussed the problem.[8] On the other hand, young evangelicals saw nothing amiss with an effort to reconcile biblical truth with evolutionary thought.[9]

Making Monkeys Out of Us

Ever since Darwin propounded the theory of evolution in his *Origin of Species,* unsaved men have seized upon it as a marvelous way in which to explain the universe and all that is in it without recourse to a sovereign God. The theory of evolution was one of the chief targets of the early fundamentalists as they did battle with the modernists. In the original volumes of *The Fundamentals* Professor George Frederick Wright of Oberlin College wrote, "The widely current doctrine of evolution which we are now compelled to combat is one which practically eliminates God from the whole creative process, and relegates man to the tender mercies of a mechanical universe, the wheels of whose machinery are left to move on without any immediate divine direction."[10]

Young evangelicals, however, desired to square the biblical accounts of creation with contemporary views, embarrassed that the creationist viewpoint was looked down upon by reputable scientists. Young evangelicals have sought ingenious ways in which to correlate the findings of unbelieving scientists with the statements of Scripture. These "green-grass" evangelicals (one term for young evangelicals) were defended by one writer in this fashion:

> What is the position of the "young evangelicals" on matters of science as related to the Bible?
>
> These "green-grass" evangelicals . . . take no strong stand as did our fundamentalist forefathers. "Green-grass" evangelicals think that the whole Christianity and science bit, including the controversy over evolution, is not really where the action is. Having had science in one way or another from the earliest grades through college, they have the feeling that science is here to stay. Why buck it?[11]

Why should we "buck" science? Because not all "science" is true science. Much of it, particularly in the area of origins, is built upon unfounded and unprovable assumptions springing from the unsaved and rebellious heart of man and not from any true scientific evidence. Matters concerning God's creative and providential activity they "willingly are ignorant of" (II Pet. 3:5). The phrase indicates a deliberate rejection of divinely revealed truth in favor of theories spun from the unregenerate human mind.

A popular position among young evangelicals was to say that the first few chapters of Genesis teach us theological truth, but not scientific truth. By using this method, nonliteralists are able to force these chapters into whatever theory of origin they may hold. Jack Rogers, a man who rejects verbal inspiration, declared, "Biblical scholars have long known that the first eleven chapters of Genesis are theological, not scientific, information."[12] In contradiction to this, however, a true scientist and Bible believer has written, "In the final analysis, all truth is one. God did not create one universe of physical reality and another of spiritual reality. The same God created all things, and His Word was given by His Holy Spirit to guide us into all truth."[13]

Removing Society's Warts

We noted in discussing the origins of the New Evangelicalism that one of the emphases was on social involvement. As time went on, however, more and more radical views proceeded from professedly evangelical sources. The young and worldly evangelicals were especially enamored with this cause. One professor at Calvin College declared that the church should be the "leaven for society" and justified the young evangelicals for "joining the liberals in causes of social concern."[14] Some went so far as to claim that the call to social action is actually a part of the gospel. Mark Hatfield, a United States senator, beseeched us to "turn to the theological problems of social revolution in the present. To do less is to concern ourselves with only half of the gospel."[15]

To defend from the New Testament the concept that social action *is included in the saving gospel of Christ* would be an impossible task. The essence of the gospel is stated in I Corinthians 15:3-4 and does not include any social action. While anyone who has the Spirit of God within would be, and should be, concerned about the plight of needy persons, to say that the mission of the church is to alleviate their miseries is to hold a position which cannot be supported from the New Testament. As a result of the church's evangelistic efforts, many social problems are lessened, but neither Christ nor the apostles mounted any organized effort to rid the Roman Empire of its social ills, which were many. It is not God's program for this age. Priority must be placed where the Lord places it—upon the spiritual needs of mankind.

On the Distaff Side

Among the young and worldly evangelicals there arose a "religious feminist" movement. Some women such as Nancy Hardesty, Sharon Gallagher, and Lucille Sider Dayton became vocal champions of evangelical "women's liberation." They unleashed their wrath upon the fundamentalist community and one of their compatriots declared, "That woman is inferior to man is an established doctrine in most Fundamentalist and Evangelical churches."[16] This statement is flawed, deliberately colored by the word "inferior." Bible-believing Christians do not hold the woman to be "inferior." There is a distinct difference between a woman's being "inferior" and a woman's being "submissive." The first word implies some lack of character or deficiency of ability, whereas the latter word involves a glad and willing response to the Word of God and its instructions concerning women.

It was among the young evangelicals that "evangelical feminists" first began to appear. Their "guru" was Paul King Jewett of Fuller Seminary. As mentioned earlier, Jewett's view was that the Pauline instructions in Ephesians and elsewhere concerning women were simply reflections of the culture Paul lived in and do not constitute divine directives for us today. He, and others, have promoted the right of female ordination to the gospel ministry.[17]

Getting on the Ecumenical Bandwagon

The original New Evangelicals were committed to the idea of infiltrating the old-line apostate denominations with bright young Bible-believers who would "turn things around." While there was some division of opinion over this among young and worldly evangelicals, many of them opted for this approach. As we have already seen, Billy Graham helped to popularize the "infiltration" approach, and it is not surprising that many of the younger evangelicals would follow him.

Eternity magazine described various evangelical renewal movements operating within the mainline denominations in an article entitled "On Not Leaving It to the Liberals."[18] One of the contributors, Tom Howard, then professor of English at Gordon College, declared that "the church needs something more than earnest individuals with their New Testaments in hand"; so he opted for the Episcopal church with its bishops who are the "appointed successors to the apostles" and for its "liturgical, sacramental life."[19]

The young evangelicals shared the same inclusivistic viewpoint of their older mentors. "The new evangelicalism is less sharply separatistic than its forerunner, fundamentalism. . . . The new evangelicals advocate remaining within the parent denomination unless it has become completely apostate. Here the conservative may exert a leavening influence, may engage in theological dialogue with his more liberal counterpart."[20]

Not only were these young and worldly evangelicals much more ecumenical than earlier fundamentalists, but some were also charismatic in their theological orientation. Their attitude is described in this way: "As we have said already, Charismatic Renewal participants understand the Pentecostal experience as transcending denominational and ideological walls while it clarifies and underscores what is authentically Christian in each tradition without demanding structural or even doctrinal changes in any church body. They are usually friendly in their attitude toward the World Council of Churches, its regional counterparts, and other ecumenical structures."[21]

In the Ivy Halls

Young evangelicals evidenced a disdain for the "Bible institute mentality" and had little use for Bible institutes and Bible colleges. To them such an education was irrelevant. They were strong on the liberal arts. They particularly disliked the "dogmatic" approach to learning. In a book authored by three professors from Wheaton College, a specimen of this outlook is found. The writers evaluated the Bible departments of fundamentalist Bible institutes and colleges:

Doctrine was taught from the perspective of learning or "memorizing" dogmatic statements. . . .

Thus the student, having spent four years in an atmosphere charged with piety, where he was trained to "smell out" the liberal and armed with the answers to the biblical and theological critics, was sent forth by the Bible department as a specimen of an educated Christian. . . . When the final evaluation of the fundamentalist movement is made, the role played by the Bible department in the growth and solidification of evangelicalism will probably be assessed as phenomenal. However, historians may rightly ask whether a true biblical Christianity or a culturally conditioned Christianity has been promoted.[22]

In reading this statement one notices immediately the contempt for the Bible-centered approach to education. It is snidely referred to as being "culturally conditioned." This is most ironic since if any education is culturally conditioned, it is New Evangelical education which "conditions" its students with the humanistic and godless culture of this world in the name of "excellence" in education.

The purpose of Christian education in the minds of many is to provide a "smorgasbord" approach. The professor is to spread out before the students all available options and opinions and the student is to take his choice among them. This is conceived of by some as a "liberal" education, developing the student's own thought processes and thus making him a "mature" person.

Traditionally, Christian schools have tried to maintain fairly high standards of personal conduct among their students. Thus there were rules to follow and discipline to be meted out if the rules were disobeyed. The young evangelicals, however, rebelled against this concept as "legalism." Their approach has been adopted by many and has led to a looseness of conduct on the campuses of many professedly Christian colleges. Many Christian colleges feel that they are cultivating maturity in the student by removing rules and regulations and allowing him to make his own choices. The vice president of one supposedly Christian college stated that his school now has an emphasis on "absolute freedom for the student" and that it has scrapped all the "Mickey Mouse rules of student life."

The liberal tendencies in theology and personal life styles have also spilled over into students' attitudes toward politics. They lament the connection they see between conservative Christianity and conservative politics (a case expounded in Richard Pierard's book *The Unequal Yoke: Evangelical Christianity and Political Conservatism*). Many younger evangelicals have become liberal social activists and are trying to cure society's ills through the practice of politics. Back in the 1970s some such zealots organized what was known as "The People's Christian Coalition." They advocated a theology of "Christian radicalism" which included the espousal of liberal political causes and an effort to wed the Christian gospel to a "prophetic denunciation" of the various societal problems of the day. They were impatient with what they viewed as a pietistic and "other-worldly" attitude on the part of older evangelicals and were desirous of attacking society's problems through corporate political action. One observer stated at the time, "The trend leftward among younger evangelicals has continued unabated."[23]

Loosening the Restrictions

The young and worldly evangelicals advocated a much freer lifestyle than had been commonly accepted among godly Christians. This view was reflected in a book by Fuller Seminary professor Lewis Smedes, *Sex for Christians*. In the chapter "Responsible Petting" he defended petting as a means of "mutual discovery."[24] In a strong statement outlining the attitudes of the young evangelicals, one writer notes,

> A third major change in contemporary evangelicalism has occurred in its cultural attitudes.
>
> Separated from the wider culture by a simple and individualistic Christian ethic characteristic of modern revivalism, the righteous life for evangelicals was most often marked by a platitudinous legalism. Smoking, drinking, dancing, theatregoing and gambling, for instance, were disallowed.
>
> Reacting against what they consider oppressive legalism, younger evangelicals have almost universally rejected these taboos as binding; and the use of four-letter words, even, is readily apparent at times in their conversation and writing. . . . It is also clear that with upward social mobility and cultural accommodation, evangelicalism as a whole—even some of the more conservative evangelical churches, colleges, seminaries, and campus ministries—no longer spend much time condemning the

older distinctive taboos that have now become socially dysfunctional, drinking in particular.[25]

This emphasis on supposed "freedom" has continued to this day. If one takes a stand against some of the vices mentioned above, one is called a legalist. Those who make such charges, however, have failed to show how sins such as drinking and smoking can be considered part of a godly life. One must determine from a study of the Word of God what constitutes a lifestyle of godliness. Certainly the consumption of alcohol, harmful as it is to the human body, could never be honestly labeled as a "godly" activity. Paul speaks of the "truth which is after godliness" (that is, which leads to godliness, Titus 1:1). There is a vital connection between theology (the truth) and one's lifestyle (godliness). Compromise in theological areas has led to compromise in lifestyles as well.

Holding Hands with Unbelievers

The basic philosophy of cooperating with unbelievers in evangelistic campaigns that was popularized by Billy Graham was embraced enthusiastically by the young and worldly evangelicals. Kenneth Strachan, then director of the Latin American Mission, conceived the notion of what was called "Evangelism-in-depth." It was an evangelistic approach geared for churches and groups in Latin America. The idea was to marshal all the church forces together to saturate Latin American countries with the gospel.

Cooperation between some mission leaders and mission agencies and the World Council of Churches began to increase as the younger evangelicals promoted that approach. In the magazine *World Vision,* published by the organization of that name, the point was made that evangelicals should cooperate with other evangelicals who are within the World Council of Churches so as to strengthen their testimony and influence within that organization.[26] In the first place, evangelicals should not be in the World Council of Churches, which is a bastion of liberal theology and practices which are hateful to God. In the second place, other evangelicals should not be assisting them in their disobedience. The "second generation" of New Evangelicals, however, had no compunction at all about working hand-in-glove with liberals.

Many young evangelicals are frank to express their desire to work more closely with theological liberals, not only in missions, but elsewhere. One sees as a bright spot on the horizon the increasing convergence of values and priorities held by Evangelicals (the emerging generation, at least) and those espoused in principle by mainstream Ecumenical liberals. This convergence can be illustrated by comparing the priorities and values of the Young Evangelicals with the goals established already in 1948 by the founding Amsterdam Assembly of the World Council of Churches.[27]

This is an amazing statement. The writer is rejoicing in the fact that evangelicals and liberals, as represented in the World Council of Churches, are drawing closer together. It is a commendation of spiritual idolatry since the "god" worshipped by the World Council of Churches is most surely a different God than we Christians worship. The great prophet Hosea was not nearly as exuberant about the departure of the people of Israel to worship false gods. Hosea roundly condemned the "spirit of whoredoms" which was in them (Hos. 5:4) and passed judgment upon their flirtation with false religion by saying, "Thou hast gone a whoring from thy God" (Hos. 9:1). If Hosea were alive today, he would be preaching the same message to modern evangelicals.

Getting Rid of Those Fences

The second generation of New Evangelicals, while not denying the necessity for some doctrinal framework, were committed to the tearing down of as many doctrinal barriers as possible. They saw doctrine as a stumbling block to evangelical ecumenicity and as a barrier to fellowship. At the thirty-fifth annual convention of the National Association of Evangelicals, some speakers spoke very strongly against requiring agreement on the doctrine of biblical inerrancy. "Pastor Don Moomaw of Bel Air Presbyterian Church in Beverly Hills, California, suggested that belief in Christ, not commitment to a doctrinal statement, is the basis of unity, and he gave Fuller Seminary a ringing endorsement in this connection. Professor Bernard Ramm of Eastern Baptist Seminary denounced an 'adversary scholarship' that 'attacks, destroys, and puts others down.' "[28] Isn't it strange that God has given us spiritual weapons dedicated to the "pulling down of strongholds" (II Cor. 10:4)? Rather sounds like an "attack mode," does it not?

The young evangelicals were declared by one to be impatient with "doctrinal questions like eternal security." He went further to state that they believe "debates over Scripture (infallibility, inerrancy) pay no great dividends. They are more experience-centered and rest their case for Christianity in the character of their encounter with Christ."[29]

This passiveness concerning debates about critical theological truth has continued to plague the church. Forgotten seems to be the warning of Paul that we not be "carried about with every wind of doctrine" (Eph. 4:14) and that we reject all that is "contrary to sound doctrine" (I Tim. 1:10). Paul exhorts again and again that we maintain "the faith" (I Tim. 6:21), "the truth" (I Tim. 3:15), and "good doctrine" (I Tim. 4:6). Jude was not adverse to "arguing" over doctrine, but he referred to it as "earnestly contending for the faith" (Jude 3).

Young Evangelicals in Action

Many of the young and worldly evangelicals became active in various parachurch organizations. An example of these is Campus Crusade, an organization majoring in ministry to college students. Bill Bright, its founder and leader, has been active over the years in promoting ecumenical efforts. He served on the executive committee of Key '73, a continent-wide evangelistic program which enlisted the cooperation of 130 denominations plus the Roman Catholic church. Campus Crusade naturally bears the image of its founder. It has been a leader in promoting ecumenical evangelism, the pragmatic approach to reaching a world for Christ.

One Christian leader spent an entire week at the headquarters of Campus Crusade, attending one of its institutes for evangelism training. This was part of his assessment of the position they took:

> During my week at Arrowhead Springs, I talked to people who were taking the Lay Institute for Evangelism Training for the express purpose of using it to increase the ministries of the local churches in apostate denominations. The United Methodist Church, the United Presbyterian Church, the American Baptist Convention, as well as liberal Episcopalians and Lutherans were represented, and not one word during the entire week of seminars and lectures ever gave any hint that converts should be warned of the mounting menace of the ecumenical movement in

America. In fact, we were specifically told "not to mention church denominations in a derogatory way."[30]

One of the programs promoted by Campus Crusade was called, "Here's Life, America." It involved thousands of volunteers from churches in given areas telephoning persons in their community and seeking to obtain "commitments to Christ" over the phone. These were then to be followed up personally. As usual Campus Crusade accepted volunteers from any and all churches regardless of their doctrinal views. An experienced fundamentalist pastor in the Chicago area was asked whether or not he had any reservations regarding this program.

> Yes, I do have reservations. When I realized the "Here's Life, America" campaign is sponsored by Campus Crusade for Christ, I recognized that this is an organization that has continually promoted ecumenical evangelism in seeking to reach a city for Christ. . . . The representative asked me if I had any questions. I asked him what type churches were asked to participate in the campaign and he answered, "All types." As a matter of fact he had that very week spoken to the Unitarian Church in the area and asked them to participate. They said they were not interested in evangelism.[31]

There is not a line in Scripture that condones such an approach to evangelism. If there are persons and churches that deny the truth of God as revealed in His Word, our duty is clear—"from such turn away" (II Tim. 3:5).

Drifting Toward Liberalism

The young and worldly evangelicals desired to retain some identification as "evangelicals," but they were moving in a direction which was taking them away from that heritage. In analyzing the movement of "worldly evangelicals" Quebedeaux remarked,

> Now . . . the evangelical left provides a better option for evangelicals who may still believe like evangelicals, but wish to behave like liberals. Furthermore, among this group there may be an increasingly large number of people who really have moved beyond evangelical belief toward liberalism. In other words, they have rejected the evangelical position intellectually (though they may not admit or even recognize it), but they still have an emotional attachment to the movement in which they were converted and nurtured.[32]

They view the mainline liberal Protestants as sisters and brothers in Christ and not as apostates to be rejected.

In wrapping up his book *The Worldly Evangelicals,* the author made an observation, the truth of which has certainly been born out:

> But the evangelical left (and more conservative evangelicals too), aided by the charismatic renewal, relational theology, a rejection of total inerrancy, broad cultural analysis, and a new ecumenical vision, are now moving toward non-evangelicals— Protestants and Catholics—with outstretched arms. At the same time many non-evangelicals themselves, aided by a fresh interest in prayer, personal and corporate Bible study, evangelism, and spirituality, are moving toward the evangelicals. In fact, we may soon see a powerful resurgence of ecumenism among evangelicals that will renew the ecumenical quest popular among Protestant liberals in the early 60's.[33]

When one begins to compromise, one drifts further and further in the wrong direction. The young and worldly evangelicals had great influence. Current evangelicalism has been greatly affected by them. The drifting has not stopped. It continues to this hour.

Notes

[1]Richard Quebedeaux, "The Evangelicals: New Trends and New Tensions," *Christianity and Crisis,* 20 September 1976, p. 197.

[2]Donald Bloesch, *The Future of Evangelical Christianity,* p. 66.

[3]Dewey Beegle, *The Inspiration of Scriptures,* p. 187.

[4]William LaSor, "Life Under Tension," in *The Authority of Scripture at Fuller,* p. 23.

[5]Carl Henry, "Conflict over Bible Inerrancy," *Christianity Today,* 7 May 1976, p. 24.

[6]G. Aiken Taylor, "Is God As Good As His Word?" *Christianity Today,* 4 February 1977, p. 2.

[7]Quebedeaux, p. 198.

[8]See especially his chapter on "Secular Man and Ultimate Concerns" in *God, Revelation, and Authority,* 1:135-51.

[9]See the discussion of evolution in an article on "Evangelicals and Evolution" by William Craig, *Journal of the Evangelical Theological Society* (Summer 1974). Another example of this approach was seen in James Buswell's article "A Creationist Interpretation of Prehistoric

Man," which was included in the volume *Evolution and Modern Thought Today*, edited by Russell Mixter.

[10]George Frederick Wright, "The Passing of Evolution," *The Fundamentals for Today*, 2:559.

[11]Bernard Ramm, "Welcome 'Green-Grass Evangelicals,' " *Eternity*, March 1974, p. 13.

[12]Jack Rogers, *Confessions of a Conservative Evangelical*, p. 126.

[13]Henry Morris, "The Bible Is a Textbook of Science," *Studies in the Bible and Science*, p. 120.

[14]Ronald Wells, "Where My Generation Parts Company," *Eternity*, May 1970.

[15]Mark Hatfield, *Conflict and Conscience*, p. 25.

[16]Richard Quebedeaux, *The Young Evangelicals*, p. 112.

[17]Paul King Jewett, "Why I Favor the Ordination of Women," *Christianity Today*, 6 June 1975.

[18]Interview Article, "On Not Leaving It to the Liberals," *Eternity*, February 1977, pp. 24ff.

[19]Tom Howard, contributor to article, "On Not Leaving It to the Liberals," p. 16.

[20]Millard Erickson, *The New Evangelical Theology*, p. 203.

[21]Richard Quebedeaux, *The New Charismatics*, p. 153.

[22]Marvin K. Mayers, Lawrence O. Richards, and Robert Webber, "Reshaping Theological Education in a Liberal Arts Setting," *Reshaping Evangelical Higher Education*, pp. 171-72.

[23]Richard Quebedeaux, "The Evangelicals: New Trends and New Tensions."

[24]Lewis Smedes, *Sex for Christians*, p. 141.

[25]Quebedeaux, "The Evangelicals: New Trends and New Tensions," p. 172.

[26]*World Vision*, October 1968.

[27]Quebedeaux, *The Young Evangelicals*, pp. 138-39.

[28]News report, *Eternity*, 1 April 1977.

[29]Ramm, p. 13.

[30]Paul Tassell, "Is Campus Crusade Scriptural?" published by Regular Baptist Press.

[31]Robert Gray, from a published interview, *Voice*, January 1977, p. 7.

[32]Quebedeaux, *The Worldly Evangelicals*, p. 166.

[33]Ibid., pp. 164-65.

5 Keeping Everybody Happy

The "New" New Evangelicalism

The New Evangelicalism has become "newer" with the passage of years. Not everyone realizes this fact or its significance. Some professedly fundamentalist schools reassure their nervous constituencies that they are opposed to the New Evangelicalism. The New Evangelicalism of which they speak, however, is that of thirty years or more ago—the brand espoused by Carl Henry, Harold Ockenga, and Edward Carnell. New Evangelicalism has come a long way since its founding. Many, while repudiating the New Evangelicalism of old, are embracing the "new" New Evangelicalism without apparently recognizing the connection between the two.

Under the Broad Umbrella

Paul warned believers not to be "carried about with every wind of doctrine, by the sleight of men, and cunning craftiness" (Eph. 4:14). This statement certainly speaks of the constant shifting that is evident in the development of human theology. It also warns us that theologians and religious teachers can be very persuasive while peddling their unscriptural wares. To distinguish between good and bad theology and methodology requires sharp spiritual discernment, a quality that seems in very short supply these days. While we are commanded to differentiate between the "spirit of truth" and the "spirit of error" (I John 4:6), it is not a popular occupation.

An Atmosphere of Change

Reflecting upon the winds of change which are blowing through religious circles these days, Hunter rightly observes that "an unsettled quality pervades the Evangelical world."[1] Clark Pinnock puts it in even stronger terms when he writes, "Evangelicals are experiencing the dizzy ferment of theological change they thought only happened to liberals."[2] Some, of course, view this as a good sign. "Away with the stilted, stuffy, and unresponsive traditional theology. Let us open the windows, let fresh air blow through, and be more innovative in our theological approaches." Such is the cry of many evangelicals today.

The fact of the matter is that many so-called evangelicals are steadily moving leftward toward a totally liberal theology. Some have already arrived there. In making such a statement, a fundamentalist is often accused of "witch-hunting" or "extremism." However, Pinnock, a perceptive nonfundamentalist and writer respected within New Evangelical circles has said it much better than a fundamentalist could: "The militant conservatives among us are not imagining everything when they charge some of us with surrendering too much in our responses to challenges of biblical criticism, evolution, feminism, political theology, and the like. There are signs that some evangelicals are on their way to becoming religious liberals, not because they choose to do so in one great step, but because in working out their ideas they have innocently covered most of the ground by smaller shifts."[3]

This is a very insightful statement and worthy of deep contemplation. It was made by one who ought to know, for he has been embarked on such a pilgrimage for many years. How true it is—apostasy creeps rather than runs into the church. Men do not start out with the intent of becoming liberals. They arrive at that point after a long journey of compromise. Apostasy is sneaky. Jude warns that "certain men crept in unawares" (Jude 4), and Peter speaks of teachers who "privily [secretly] shall bring in damnable heresies" (II Pet. 2:1).

The scene reminds one of the description some gave years ago of Karl Barth's theology, that it was "theology on the wing" because you never knew where it was going to land next. After giving a rather extensive list of individuals, institutions, and organizations that are New Evangelical, Bloesch observes, "What is important to recognize is that every person and fellowship mentioned in this section . . . is moving. While some may be neoevangelical or neofundamentalist in this period, in another few years they may belong more properly in another category."[4] Another observer indicates, "It is also reasonable to predict that the Evangelical world view will undergo still further mutations that will make it even less similar to the historical faith than it already is."[5]

Both of these men are saying that evangelicalism is changing. But is it changing for the better? Some would say yes. However, one astute observer of the evangelical scene who had contacts and ministry in a wide variety of settings said no. Here are the comments of Francis Schaeffer in his book, *The Great Evangelical Disaster:*

> *Within the evangelical circles things are moving rapidly in the direction of what happened fifty years ago in the denominations.*
> . . . There is a growing infiltration of humanistic ideas into the theology and practice. There is a growing acceptance of pluralism and accommodation. And what has been the response of the evangelical leadership? Overwhelmingly it has been to keep silent, to let the slide go further and further, to paper over the differences. Here again we see the great evangelical disaster— the failure of evangelical leadership to take a stand really on anything that would stand decisively over against the relativistic side of our culture.[6]

Some fundamentalists, particularly younger ones, look somewhat longingly at the mushrooming churches of certain New Evangelicals, wish their churches were growing similarly, and begin to wonder whether they should "get into the swing of things" and begin moving with the tide. Such temptations should be countered by a "look at the Book." True, solid, and scriptural theology is not characterized by movement but by stability. "For ever, O Lord, thy word is settled in heaven" (Ps. 119:89). We are to "continue in the faith grounded and settled, and be not moved away from the hope of the gospel" (Col. 1:23). Paul tells us to "hold fast the form of sound words" (II Tim. 1:13). We are to "contend for the faith" (Jude 3), which indicates that we are to defend the historic and unchangeable Christian faith and not allow charlatans to move us from it.

Younger pastors and believers need to realize that change does not necessarily mean progress. The divinely revealed "faith of our fathers" should not be changed. The emphasis of the New Testament is upon the preservation of the faith, not upon the redevelopment of it. We see no exhortations in Scripture to "contextualize the faith." "The faith" is that body of doctrine revealed to us by God and inscripturated in our Bibles. It does not need changing or improvement. It is eternal and dependable.

Same Animal—New Designation

Part of the current confusion regarding New Evangelicalism stems from the fact that there is now little difference between evangelicalism and New Evangelicalism. The principles of the original New Evangelicalism have become so universally accepted by those who refer to themselves as evangelicals that any distinctions which might have been made years ago are all but lost. It is no doubt true to state that "Ockenga's designation of the new movement as 'New or Neo-Evangelical' was abbreviated to 'Evangelical.' . . . Thus today we speak of this branch of conservative Christianity simply as the Evangelical movement."[7] As we noted earlier, the young and worldly evangelicals took positions that embarrassed even the founders of the New Evangelicalism. "The movement got far beyond their control and grew as the result of forces never anticipated in their plans."[8]

Few people today characterize themselves by the term New Evangelical. That does not mean, however, that there are no New Evangelicals. It merely means that the nomenclature has been shortened. It is perhaps all the more dangerous because it does not have any special name, but simply sails under the time-honored word—*evangelical.*

Your Rift Is Showing

Young people often carry ideas way beyond their elders, and students tend to become more radical than their teachers. Francis Bacon said that "young men, in the conduct and management of actions, embrace more than they can hold, stir more than they can quiet, fly to the end without consideration of the means and degrees, and pursue absurdly some few principles which they have chanced upon."[9]

Certainly this has occurred within New Evangelicalism. The "right wing" New Evangelicals (the older, more conservative members) are dismayed at the distance which the "left wing" (the younger, more radical members) have traveled.

The Concerns of the "Right Wing"

Carl Henry, one of the original founders of the New Evangelicalism, made some significant observations about the "new" New Evangelicalism. In reacting to Hunter's volume *Evangelicalism:*

The Coming Generation, Henry expressed alarm. Hunter's book contained surveys made on the campuses of leading evangelical colleges in America, surveys that revealed a very radical departure from the norms of orthodoxy. Henry remarked:

> When one focuses not on marginal, but on centrally important control, the evangelical campuses surveyed, as a group, do reflect disconcerting theological deterioration. Moreover, in my graduate teaching on numerous seminary campuses, I have confirmed to my own satisfaction the accuracy of Hunter's indications, for example, that even on some of the best evangelical college campuses, some professors have taught their students that Jesus Christ is not the sole ground of human acceptance by God and the entire human race need not have descended from Adam.[10]

Carl Henry has a right to be concerned. The early compromises of New Evangelicalism have resulted in a terrifying harvest among the second and third generations.

Harold Lindsell, as was already mentioned, was an early star in the New Evangelical galaxy. A professor at Fuller Seminary for a while, he then became editor of the prestigious New Evangelical periodical, *Christianity Today.* He is a "blue chip" New Evangelical. Read carefully, then, this astounding admission from his pen:

> I must regretfully conclude that the term *evangelical* has become so debased that it has lost its usefulness. Decades ago when the label *new evangelical* was coined its viability was based upon one positive and one negative aspect. On the positive side it took over without change the basic theological heritage of fundamentalism. By this I mean its commitment to historic orthodoxy as derived from the New Testament, and the Reformation, and expressed in the various creeds of Christendom since then. . . . On the negative side, it dispensed with the traditional fundamentalist sociology, i.e., fundamentalism's understanding of the relationship of the Christian to the world. . . . The *new evangelical* turned from fundamentalism's sociology to positive interaction with the world and engagement on the intellectual level with liberal theological education. . . . Maybe it would be better to accept the term *fundamentalist* with all of the pejoratives attached to it by its detractors.[11]

Amazing! One of the architects of the New Evangelicalism is now saying that the term *evangelical* is suspect. What made it suspect? The continuing drift and increasing compromise evident among those who bear the name.

The Division Among New Evangelicals

Donald Bloesch, in his penetrating analysis of the evangelical situation found in his book *The Future of Evangelical Christianity,* attempts to delineate the "right-wingers" and the "left-wingers" among the evangelicals. He sees at least two important issues which tend to divide them: (1) the nature of biblical inspiration, and (2) the proper approach to biblical interpretation.[12] More will be said about those issues in a later discussion.

Among seminaries that he says are more open to the new mood but are still influenced by fundamentalism he lists

Trinity Seminary
Denver Theological Seminary
Covenant Theological Seminary
Talbot Theological Seminary

That the institutions named are still in any measure "influenced by fundamentalism" is certainly open to question, but these schools just listed are the schools Bloesch would view as on the "right wing" of the evangelical spectrum and thus more conservative than others. His candidates for the "left wing" would be

Fuller Theological Seminary
Gordon-Conwell Seminary
Bethel Theological Seminary
Regent College
Eastern Mennonite Seminary
Eastern Baptist Theological Seminary
North Park Theological Seminary

Bloesch also gives a classification of Christian publishing houses. The "left wing" are as follows:

William B. Eerdmans Publishing Company
Inter-Varsity Press
Fleming Revell
Word Books

The "right wing" would be represented in the following:

Zondervan Publishing House
Thomas Nelson
Baker Book House
Tyndale House Publishers

Of the Christian periodicals which he classifies, the following he views as "left wing":

Christian Scholar's Review
United Evangelical Action
The Evangelical Quarterly
Evangelical Newsletter

On the right would be

Journal of the Evangelical Theological Society
The Westminster Theological Journal
Trinity Journal

In evaluating New Evangelical leaders he places the following on the right wing: Francis Schaeffer, R. C. Sproul, James Boice, James Packer, Harold O. J. Brown, John Gerstner, John Warwick Montgomery, and Harold Lindsell. He also mentions in this group Carl Henry, Roger Nicole, John Stott, Vernon Grounds, and Kenneth Kantzer. The separating issue for Bloesch is the question of *inerrancy.* The above-mentioned would hold to *inerrancy* whereas the left wing group would use the term *infallibility,* believing that the Scriptures are correct in their teaching of doctrine but not in other areas of thought. Among these left-wingers would be found Clark Pinnock, F. F. Bruce, Bernard Ramm, Bruce Metzger, George Eldon Ladd, Jack Rogers, James Daane, Paul Jewett, Lewis Smedes, and others.

Two Watershed Issues

As mentioned earlier, two important issues divide the two wings of New Evangelicalism: (1) inspiration and (2) interpretation. Bloesch himself, who has made such a study of the two "wings" of the movement, is decidedly on the weaker side in this debate. To him the Bible is "a divinely-appointed channel, a mirror, or a visible sign of divine revelation."[13] Seeking to escape the Warfield-Hodge, old Princeton Seminary emphasis which is so abhorrent to many of these "new" New Evangelicals, Bloesch embraces a position perilously close to neo-orthodoxy. It is no wonder he commends the neo-orthodox theologians for their attempt "to recover the dynamic character of divine revelation."[14] Bloesch's position, which would be characteristic of the left-wing New Evangelical, would be as follows:

1. Fundamentalism has placed too much emphasis upon the words of Scripture to the neglect of meaning, truth, and power.

2. The objective nature of truth is compromised by stating that truth is conformity to the will and purpose of God, and not necessarily connected to propositional statements.

3. What we may call error today was not viewed as error by the biblical authors nor by those living in earlier and other cultures. We should not apply a stricter view of error to the Bible.[15]

In 1965, while professor of theology at Bethel Theological Seminary in St. Paul, Minnesota, Clarence Bass gave a workshop at Founder's Week (February 16, 1965). His subject was "The Relation Between Inspiration and Inerrancy." In that lecture Bass declared that the view of inerrancy held by the modern fundamentalist is recent in origin and was not held by orthodox scholars of earlier ages. James Hollowood, then Executive Secretary of the Minnesota Baptist Convention, asked Bass for clarification of his views. In a letter to Hollowood on September 16, 1966, Bass said, "That is to say I clearly distinguish between inspiration as a Biblical doctrine and inerrancy as a logical correlative."[16] In other words, the Bible can be inspired, but not inerrant.

Back when Fuller Seminary changed its doctrinal statement, it became fashionable among many New Evangelicals to distinguish between *inerrancy* (which they did not believe) and *infallibility* (which they professed to believe). That distinction is still maintained by some. What they mean is that the Bible does contain errors in noncrucial areas such as geography, history, and numerology, but that it is still reliable (infallible) when it comes to the important and critical doctrines which it teaches. One summarizes the situation in this way:

> With the inroads of modern science and biblical criticism into American evangelical theological circles . . . the total inerrancy position has become increasingly difficult to maintain. Thus a doctrine of "limited inerrancy" began to be promulgated during the 1960's that was finally, in 1972, incorporated into the

statement of faith held by Fuller Theological Seminary, evangelicalism's most prestigious graduate school of theology.

This position—affirming that Scripture is inerrant or infallible in its teaching on matters of faith and conduct but not necessarily in all its assertions concerning history and the cosmos—is gradually becoming ascendant among the most highly respected evangelical theologians. They feel strongly that the doctrine of limited inerrancy both preserves the Bible's authority and makes feasible the use of the higher-critical method in studying its contents.[17]

What a sad day it is when professedly evangelical theologians will scuttle the view of inspiration which the Bible itself teaches so they can employ a Bible-study method spawned in the minds of rank unbelievers who hate the Word of God and its message! The higher-critical method coveted by the New Evangelicals is nothing more than a humanistic, rationalistic approach to Scripture.

Clark Pinnock represents "limited inerrantists" when he says that the Bible "*contains* errors but teaches none."[18] He means to say that not all of the Bible's presentation is "teaching," that is, doctrinal instruction. David Hubbard, president of Fuller Seminary, proposes that we should discard the term "inerrancy" and use only the term "infallibility."[19] In a different way he is advocating the same thing as Pinnock.

Many New Evangelicals are charismatics or are influenced by the charismatic movement. Charismatics emphasize special spiritual experiences that they claim are vital to the Christian life. Many of them believe that God is giving extrabiblical revelation today and see the gift of prophecy as the divine communication of truth apart from the Scriptures. If this be true, then it is obvious that the Scriptures do not give us a final revelation. Such a viewpoint is indeed a dangerous one and, we believe, contrary to both Scripture and the historic position of orthodox Christianity. The question of miracles is also pertinent to a discussion of the sufficiency of Scripture. If miracles are needed, and are indeed being performed today, then the Bible is not sufficient; other revelation is needed, revelation being given in the form of miracles. Many Christians are claiming to have wondrous experiences today, and in many cases these experiences take authoritative precedence over the Bible. "It is absolutely necessary to allow the Bible to judge every experience. If there is not clear teaching in the Bible to support a practice, it should

101

not be adopted by the church today, *regardless of how beautiful and seemingly miraculous the experiences are that it produces.*"[20]

This age of grace is not the age of miracles. No Bible-believing Christian doubts the ability of God to perform miracles; however, it is not part of His program today to do so. God authenticated the ministry of the apostles with "signs and wonders, and with divers miracles" (Heb. 2:4), but when the apostolic age concluded, the accompanying signs ceased.

What Does the Bible Really Say?

The authority of the Bible is being undermined by spurious methods of interpretation. Schaeffer was absolutely right when he wrote, "The Bible is made to say only that which echoes the surrounding culture at our moment of history. *The Bible is bent to the culture instead of the Bible judging our society and culture.*"[21] Professedly evangelical scholars today can make the Bible say almost anything they want it to say simply by adopting erroneous methods of interpretation.

Hunter discusses three reasons that he believes present-day conservatives are no longer capable of maintaining the traditional boundaries of orthodoxy. The second reason he gives has to do with biblical interpretation.

> The second reason can only be inferred, but the logic and the evidence are compelling. It is that an increasing number of Evangelicals no longer really believe in the sanctity of these symbolic boundaries. . . . Once their belief that the central facts (carried by the traditions and taught by the churches) are facts in the most literal and absolute sense is weakened, traditional religion begins to disintegrate. The most important case in point is the place of Scriptures. When it is allowed, as it is increasingly so in Evangelicalism, to interpret the Bible subjectivistically and to see portions of Scripture as symbolic or nonbinding, the Scriptures are divested of their authority to compel obedience. They may still inspire, but they are substantially disarmed.[22]

In other words, if, as do many evangelical Bible teachers, one reads in Ephesians 5:22, "Wives, submit yourselves unto your own husbands," one simply says, "That does not constitute a command from God; it merely represents Paul's rabbinic and masculine bias. We can forget it." Interpretation becomes a convenient way to dispose of unliked and unwanted Scriptures. This is what Clark refers to when he complains about evangelicals who play loose with the Scriptures. "More serious, in my opinion, are the indirect ways of using exegesis to undermine the authority of scripture, especially in its support of distinctively Christian way of life."[23] We believe he is referring here to attempts in recent years by so-called evangelical scholars to justify lifestyles such as homosexuality as "Christian."

The "Evangelical Megashift"

Tremendous changes are taking place in evangelicalism as a whole. Robert Brow took a look at the scene and came up with several leading features of what he calls the "new-model" evangelicalism. It should be remembered in perusing his ideas that not all evangelicals would agree with every point. However, his observations certainly spell out the direction in which many are moving. Here is a summary of what he feels are characteristics that are coming to the fore within the New Evangelicalism.

1. God is seen as a warm Father instead of a strict Judge. This includes for many the rejection of the historic doctrine of eternal hell.

2. Faith is more of a constant looking in the right direction than a momentary decision.[24]

3. God's wrath should be thought of, not as angry punishment, but as bad consequences which result from poor behavior. "So wrath is more like a loving encouragement or rebuke to help us into (or keep us in) the fold. New-model evangelicals shrink from using the terrors of hell to scare people into making a decision."[25]

4. Sin does not condemn us to hell. It just brings forth the fatherly care of God with a view to discipline and correction.

5. The church is not a "stockade for the saved or an agency to save souls" but an institution "to offer the resources of the Spirit to all who want to learn how to love and enjoy God and their neighbors."[26]

6. Missions is not an attempt to rescue lost heathen from hell. It rather involves "enrolling by baptism any who want to learn and training them, forming them into church families where the Spirit will teach them all that Jesus taught."[27]

7. Christ saves through His eternal life and not merely through the cross.

On this seventh point, note the following statement:

> New-model evangelicals . . . view the Son of God as eternally
> both Lord and Servant, Shepherd and Lamb. He did not become
> Lamb simply when He was put on the cross. His identity as Lamb
> was eternal in the sense that he was already absorbing our sin
> and its consequences from the time the first creatures were made
> in the image of God. This means the cross was not a judicial
> payment, but the visible expression in a space-time body of his
> eternal nature as Son.[28]

To refute all the error included in this summary would require
more time than we can devote in this book. Needless to say, a
first-year student of theology could readily see the fallacies from a
biblical standpoint. As we have said, not all New Evangelicals
would agree with Brow, but the fact that his article could be
published in the leading New Evangelical magazine, *Christianity
Today,* is proof that "something is rotten in Denmark."

Looking at the "New Look"

How does one recognize the New Evangelicalism in its more
up-to-date dress?

The Spirit of "Niceness"

Franky Schaeffer put it this way: "The clear, loud call for
accommodation comes wrapped in the name of the Gospel of
Niceness. Sin as the source of all human problems is banished and
a call for repentance is rarely made."[29] Evangelicalism today is
consumed with relationalism, the fine art of getting along with
people. Bruce Larson, a leading New Evangelical author himself,
advises us that "the quality and scope of relationships and the
ability and willingness to relate are marks of orthodoxy rather than
doctrine."[30] In other words, the emphasis in theology becomes
relational and not conceptual. This tendency, by the way, accounts
for a major shift in expectations of the average church member
toward the ministry of the pastor. Many want the pastor to center
his preaching around "how to" themes rather than doctrinal themes.
More will be said about this later.

The attitude of evangelicals today is, "Let's not offend anyone.
Let's preach the gospel in such a way as to be well-thought-of by
the unsaved world." "To begin with, most Evangelicals tacitly
recognize that Protestant hegemony in America has given way to a

potpourri of religious belief systems that itself is girded by a strong liberal code of religious tolerance. . . . In response, Evangelicalism has adopted a social posture that pleads, 'Don't take offense, but here is the truth.' It is a demeanor of propriety, gentility, and sociability."[31]

This spirit of gentility, of "niceness," permeates evangelicalism. It affects the approach which evangelicals take toward the presentation of the gospel and their general attitude toward cardinal doctrines of Scripture. "The civilizing process entails a deemphasis of Evangelicalism's more offensive aspects: the notions of inherent evil, sinful conduct and lifestyles, the wrath of a righteous and jealous God, and eternal agony and death in hell."[32] The popular pastor, Chuck Swindoll, says, "When there is a grace-awakening ministry there is an absence of dogmatism and Bible-bashing. . . . There is a spirit of openness."[33]

One of the original founders of the New Evangelicalism, Carl Henry, is not impressed with the "progress" which has been made. He is alarmed by certain trends and speaks out against them.

> In contrast to inclusive modernism, evangelical spokesmen have hesitated to declare all nonbiblical religions false. They have spoken rather in terms of the "superiority" of evangelical orthodoxy. In short, in deference to the growing mood of tolerance and for the sake of civility in dialogue, the Christian belief was packaged for greater marketability. References to eschatological damnation and to hell as the final destiny of the impenitent wicked were evaded, abridged, or introduced semi-apologetically. The term "heresy" vanished from inter-religious dialogue.[34]

What saith the Scriptures? Our Lord did not seem to concern Himself with the gospel of niceness when He thundered, "Woe unto you, scribes and Pharisees, hypocrites" (Matt. 23:14 et al.). Paul was not being very nice when he indicted his fellow Jews with the crucifixion of Jesus and declared that "wrath is come upon them to the uttermost" (I Thess. 2:14-16). No thought of "helpful dialogue" seemed to be in the apostle's mind when he emphatically denounced those who preached a false gospel as those who would be "accursed" (Gal. 1:9). In summary, the method of presenting biblical truth as exemplified by the apostles, the founders of the church, does not square with the "new look" in evangelicalism. Early Christians did not specialize in making everyone feel comfortable. They spoke the truth in the power of the Spirit, with love but also with clarity and forcefulness. They pulled no punches.

A Nose of Wax

Noses of wax can be twisted to any shape desired. With a nose of wax you can satisfy the desires of almost anyone for a "revised countenance." Such a nose can be accommodated to almost any desired configuration.

New Evangelicalism began with the spirit of accommodation. "Let's not be confronters, but rather builders. Let us see how much common ground we occupy along with the liberals and neo-orthodox. Let's try to draw a wider circle and include as many as possible rather than a narrower circle which excludes many." Of course, in order to do that one must compromise. The compromise begins with small matters, but, sadly, grows to include large and important matters. Pride of intellect has characterized the New Evangelicalism from the beginning.

> Evangelicalism has become respectable. To some extent, this respectability may have been bought at a price. . . . Partly as a consequence of their accommodation to existing cultural standards as befitting the new place many Evangelicals hold in society, one can identify in recent years a certain openness with respect to life-style standards, politics, and theological orientation, even with regard to biblical inerrancy.[35]

Early New Evangelicals, particularly the schoolmen and scholars among them, became restive with what they perceived to be their isolated position in society, especially in religious society. They longed to have more recognition, to have their articles and books published by "respectable" companies, and to be looked up to as authentic scholars. Bloesch is certainly on target when he writes, "Much of the accommodation of today, as of yesterday, is rooted in the concern to make the faith palatable or desirable to its cultured despisers."[36] Dangerous business this! Trying to shape the "faith of our fathers" into a system that will be viewed by a godless, rationalistic world as acceptable is not a scriptural approach.

Some have contrasted what they call "confessional theology" with "revisionist theology." By "confessional" they mean "historic orthodoxy." By "revisionist" they mean the updated, New Evangelical theology which seeks to conform the Word of God to modern tastes. Revisionist theology "is bent on revising or updating the life and thought of the church in the light of the new world consciousness. . . . It represents an accommodation to the *Zeitgeist* (the spirit of the times)."[37]

What is the problem here? It is simply this: many modern evangelicals have become embarrassed to be seen carrying the cross. They bridle at the thought of having to be rejected and sneered at by the unbelieving world. They long to have a "place in the sun." They do not relish the experience of being looked down upon as "red-necked bigots" and "Bible thumpers." For this reason they are attempting to "dress up" the Christian faith. Hunter notes that if modern evangelicals would continue to preach and practice their faith as did their forefathers, they would be greatly hampered in their goal of reaching the world around them. Listen to this amazing and heart-rending admission:

> In short, to reinforce the traditional symbolic boundaries of orthodox Protestantism would require Evangelicals to operate defiantly against these social and cultural restraints. They would have to publicly invoke and rigorously apply the "harsher" and more "offensive" symbols of their faith. In practical terms this would mean publicly labeling some people sinners, heretics, or infidels; all, though, in danger of God's judgment and eternal punishment. To do so would undoubtedly generate untoward consequences. They would risk offending and alienating not only non-Evangelicals (those they hope to win over to the faith), but their own following as well.[38]

In our wildest imaginings, we cannot conceive of the Apostle Paul or any of the other apostles maintaining such a position as here described. Did Stephen, the first Christian martyr, evaluate the desires of his audience, weigh the consequences of negative remarks, and decide in favor of a more moderate approach? He did nothing of the sort. Facing an antagonistic audience of Jewish hearers, he told them that they were "stiffnecked and uncircumcised in heart and ears" and that they were resisters of the Holy Spirit (Acts 7:51). As a result the crowd were "cut to the heart, and they gnashed on him with their teeth" (Acts 7:54). Stephen would have made a poor twentieth-century evangelical. If asked how it is that an evangelical view of life seems to command a wider popular support today than perhaps it once did, we should listen to this observation: "An answer is to be found in a historical shift in Evangelicalism's cultural demeanor. This has entailed a softening and polishing of the more hard-line and barbed elements of the orthodox Protestant world view. Although at its doctrinal core this world view remains essentially unchanged, it has been culturally edited to give it the qualities of sociability and gentility. . . . It has resulted from a modified accommodation to the cultural plurality of modernity."[39]

Similar warnings even from those who would not be considered "wild-eyed fundamentalists" could be multiplied on these pages. One nonfundamentalist writer declares that "compromise, or 'accommodation,' is the most formidable threat to evangelicalism today."[40] In another place he says, "We rationalize our attitudes and actions by declaring that new times require new approaches. And more than a few of us are willing to embrace and identify with the depraved and deprived value systems of today's society, simply because our society extends the warm hand of friendship and acceptance. *It feels so good to be admired*" (emphasis added).[41]

What is the call of Christ to His disciples? "If any man will come after me, let him deny himself, and take up his cross, and follow me" (Matt. 16:24). People carrying crosses are not popular. A cross alienates. A cross slays. Worldlings don't want crosses. And what else did Christ say? "If the world hate you, ye know that it hated me before it hated you. If ye were of the world, the world would love his own: but because ye are not of the world, but I have chosen you out of the world, therefore the world hateth you" (John 15:18-19). Would you call this a spirit of accommodation?

Evangelical Feminism

In recent years we have seen a rise of radical feminism which has had some articulate and strident advocates, both men and women. In the world such strong and outspoken persons as Mary Daly have forwarded the feminist agenda with great force. The Equal Rights Amendment was debated for years, but it never became the law of the land. Nevertheless, the radical feminists have made much headway.

One, of course, could expect the unsaved world to get on the feminist bandwagon since they are spiritually blind and have no allegiance to the authority of the Word of God. One is taken aback, however, to witness those who claim to be evangelicals propounding many of the same ideas that are held by the ungodly. The development of so-called evangelical feminism began with the rise of the young and worldly evangelicals back in the 1970s. In 1976 Quebedeaux observed:

> The women's movement has made substantial gains within all these subgroups. Most young evangelicals accept the use of the inclusive language, the ordination of women, egalitarian marriage and the Equal Rights Amendment. . . . Though all evangelical feminists end up in the same place scripturally, the more conservative part (limited inerrancy types) stands on the principle that the Bible does not teach what it has been assumed to teach about the subordinate role of women in the church and society; rather the *interpretation* of Scripture has been culturally conditioned. The radical party, however, following Jewett, argues simply that the New Testament conveys liberation for all people and was not intended to oppress modern women by imposing on them a first-century patriarchal family structure. St. Paul . . . when he demands the subordination of women to men . . . is wrong.[42]

Those who call themselves evangelical feminists declare that historic, orthodox theology was "thought up" by males and reflects their biases. Eloise Fraser, a theology professor at Eastern Baptist Seminary at the time of writing, complains that evangelical theologians claim they are doing their theology "from above," from the standpoint of divine revelation. Fraser says, however, that "most theology has been written out of the male's experience of God, the world, and others."[43] She is much upset about what she calls "the paternalistic teaching in our seminaries" which she says "crushes theological creativity because of the paternalistic need to maintain control over people's minds."[44] The truth of the matter is, we have far too much "theological creativity" which takes people outside the bounds of Holy Scripture. We need less human *creativity* and more submission to the *authority* of God's Book. Evangelical feminism is a result of human creativity and not a result of scriptural exegesis.

Whence has come this new and wondrous system known as evangelical feminism? How is it that none of the great and respected exegetes of the church through all these centuries have uncovered these new "truths"? Why is evangelical feminism a late-twentieth-century phenomenon? Is it because we now have scholars more able

109

and more holy with greater spiritual insight than those before them? No, it is because feminism has become popular in the world and some evangelicals now wish to make the church "modern," "up-to-date," and "relevant." The rise of evangelical feminism coincides with the rise of worldly feminism. Its teachings were not found in the Bible but in the matrix of the godless society around us. We are aware that effort has been made in recent years by proponents of evangelical feminism to justify their views from Scripture, but such efforts were never made until some found it necessary to bring the world's concept of the role of women into the church. Then some scriptural defense must be found for it so as to make it palatable to Christians, who are supposed to accept the Bible as the final authority. "Some evangelical leaders, in fact, have changed their views about inerrancy as a direct consequence of trying to come to terms with feminism. There is no other word for this than accommodation. It is a direct and deliberate bending of the Bible to conform to the world spirit of our age at the point where the modern spirit conflicts with what the Bible teaches."[45]

If evangelicals were not supposed to be champions of biblical authority, the problem would not be nearly as bad. One writer points out that passages such as Ephesians 5 and I Timothy 2 which, for many centuries, have been understood by evangelical exegetes to teach the godly submission of women, are now proving to be problem passages for evangelical feminists. In speaking of these passages and their teaching, one writer notes, "The inference of sexual subordination and inferiority is hardly concealed. What makes these passages especially 'difficult' (as one Evangelical feminist euphemistically put it) is the Evangelical commitment to biblical literalism and inerrancy. Without that commitment, such 'problem verses' present little problem at all. They can easily be ignored or relativized by claiming that these Scriptures simply reflect the cultural setting of the writer and not the transcendent truths."[46] As a matter of fact, this is just the way many modern evangelicals handle the matter. The central truths, say they, have been cluttered up by transmission through the minds of first-century male chauvinists (the apostles), and we who have greater insight in the twentieth century need to strip away the clutter and find the lasting truths.

The Bible is clear. God made man and woman to be separate, God-honoring persons, submissive to His Word, and productive in the roles assigned. The Bible does not teach the "inferiority" of women, and true biblical theologians have never held that. God made for man a woman to be, literally, "a helper suitable for him" (Gen. 2:18). Christian women are to emulate the godly women of old and to display that "meek and quiet spirit, which is in the sight of God of great price" (I Pet. 3:4). Saved women are to be "discreet, chaste, keepers at home, good, obedient to their own husbands" (Titus 2:5). "Favour is deceitful, and beauty is vain: but a woman that feareth the Lord, she shall be praised" (Prov. 31:30). None of these descriptions seem to fit the ideal woman as set forth by the evangelical feminists. Many of these are strident, "pushy," and insistent upon their "rights." A godly woman is not so.

Hash That's Not So Heavenly

When I was growing up, my family was not well-to-do. We had to make dollars stretch. To this end, my mother was very skilled at using up all the leftovers of the week's meals. She would proudly mix together many diverse ingredients, add seasonings, and serve her famous "heavenly hash." What was in it? Who knew? You just ate it and thanked the Lord you had something to eat. More and more "theological hash" is being served in generous helpings today.

Years ago one of the groups that preceded the World Council of Churches had for its slogan "Doctrine divides; service unites." While not all evangelicals would agree totally with the thrust of that saying, it nevertheless reflects an attitude which is very prevalent among evangelicals. When I was pastoring in a midwestern city, a local charismatic pastor came in to see our school administrator. Commenting on the current religious scene he said, "What we need to do is just forget all this doctrine-stuff, and just love Jesus." It sounds nice, doesn't it? We don't need doctrine—just Jesus. But who, pray tell, is Jesus? The moment you seek to answer that question you have entered the realm of doctrine.

A certain shallowness has developed in evangelical circles across the years. This is not to say that there are none who are concerned about theology, but Carl Henry noted that as evangelicalism grew, "serious theology received little attention. . . . Youth for Christ, for example, was far more prone to send up a 'cheer for

Jesus' than to repeat the Apostles' Creed."[47] Bloesch complains that "conspicuous in American church life in particular is the dissipation of doctrinal and apostolic substance. There is a preoccupation with the cultivation of the inner life and holistic salvation but faithfulness to the apostolic faith . . . is dismally lacking."[48] In discussing the evolution of the present-day Fuller Theological Seminary, Roberta Hestenes, who once taught there, said that the purpose of a seminary is not merely the development of the intellect, but the nurturing of a spirit of service, hence "spiritual formation was probably more important than theological precision."[49] But how can one have spiritual growth without theological growth, that is, a deepening of one's understanding of doctrine? Peter admonishes us to "grow in grace, and in the knowledge of our Lord and Saviour Jesus Christ" (II Pet. 3:18). "Growing" and "knowledge" go together. "Knowledge" involves the increasing grasp of doctrinal truth. If any institution should be dedicated to "precise theology," it should surely be a theological seminary.

Popular today is the concept that love is the most important ingredient in the Christian life. By love is generally meant a soft tolerance toward error, even gross error, and a gentle spirit of acceptance toward any and all who call themselves evangelicals. It is this attitude which has allowed the charismatic teachings to become such a prominent feature of the contemporary church. Christian leaders will say, "I am not a charismatic personally, but the charismatic movement has done a lot of good, and we ought not to condemn it. We are to love the brethren." So, in the name of love, all manner of false teaching is condoned. We need to listen to Martin Luther who wrote, "Doctrine is not ours but God's. . . . Therefore, we may not yield or change even one tittle of it. . . . Accursed be that love which is preserved to the detriment of the doctrine of faith. . . . For doctrine is our sole light which . . . shows us the way to heaven. If it becomes wobbly in one part, it must necessarily become wobbly altogether. When that happens, love cannot help us."[50]

Some may note, however, that there are many articles being written about doctrine, and many discussions being held. We note two things in response: (1) these discussions, by and large, are outside the sphere of the average believer in a local church, and (2) those who are discussing in many cases are not willing to say that a particular view is the right and only view. It is an "option" or an "alternative viewpoint." In many cases there is a lack of real conviction, coupled with a reluctance to brand some other evangelical's view as wrong. The charismatic movement has added to this problem since many of them promote the idea that "Spirit baptism" is the catalyst that brings everyone together, and other doctrinal differences can be overlooked. Martyn Lloyd-Jones was sensitive to this problem and concerned about it while he still lived. "This is one of the great problems facing all of us as evangelical Christians at the present time, because there are evangelical people who are talking like this now: they say that doctrine does not matter. In other words, they say that you can have this true unity in spite of profound disagreement concerning vital and essential doctrines."[51]

We can all thank God that this denigration of doctrine was not the attitude of Paul. Not for one moment did he ignore or downplay precious Bible truth while pretending to practice Christian love. He commanded sound doctrine to be taught. He also warned, "If any man teach otherwise, and consent not to wholesome words . . . and to the doctrine which is according to godliness; he is proud, knowing nothing" (I Tim. 6:3-4). Pastors are "to put the brethren in remembrance of these things" so that they will be "nourished up in the words of faith and of good doctrine" (I Tim. 4:6). They are to give special attention "to reading, to exhortation, to doctrine" (I Tim. 4:13).

The Devil in the Choir Loft

The doctrinal slide about which we have been speaking is also apparent in the realm of Christian music. The mushiness and shallowness of theology so evident in the professing church today is certainly plainly seen in that phenomenon known as "Contemporary Christian Music." Horton has a very astute observation concerning this:

> In other words, the shift . . . is, generally speaking, a change in emphasis from a God-centered, objective, historical faith that is for me, but outside of me, to a man-centered, subjective, existential faith that is almost exclusively concerned with personal experiences with the Spirit or with Jesus.
>
> This shift is reflected in the comment, "Let's just love Jesus—theology just gets in the way."[52]

The Contemporary Christian Music so loved by large numbers of evangelicals today is witness to the theological deterioration of the church. Spiritual Christians are aghast at the frothy, wild, undisciplined, and earthly music sung and played by so-called Christian rock groups. There is more than an age gap here. There is a difference between that which is spiritual and that which is fleshly. "The older music was essentially intellectual; it was located in the mind and in the feelings known to the mind; the new music rocks the whole body and penetrates the soul."[53] Reich here was contrasting secular, classical music and modern rock, but the same thing could be said for the distinction between traditional Christian music and the "modern beat." This same thought was underscored by Robert Pattison in his book *The Triumph of Vulgarity: Rock Music in the Mirror of Romanticism*. He said, "Rock lyrics are suffused with the language of emotion: need, want, and feel are the building blocks of its abstract vocabulary. Logic and reason are everywhere associated with the loss of youth and death of vitality."[54]

The rock music culture of our day definitely has been baptized and has put on the church choir robes. Years ago we began to hear the cry, "You can't reach the young people unless you employ their favorite musical styles." When did bald pragmatism become the standard for the church's outreach? Pastors and church leaders became nervous and decided they would have to compete with the secular rock culture. Thus they became "the entrepreneurs of emotional stimulation. Once God becomes a commodity for self-gratification, his fortunes depend on the vagaries of the emotional marketplace."[55]

The major thrust of modern popular Christian music is experience. It fits in with the self-centered culture of the day in which persons concentrate on "meeting their needs." "Rock was a music made to order for this new cultural vision. . . . It had a natural appeal to youth, who enjoy noisy, emotional, and sensual displays. But it also fulfilled the prescription of many sophisticated Western adults for whom the tradition of high culture has become exhausted, and who were looking for liberation in experience."[56] Although music rightly can reflect emotions, it must never be merely emotional. It must be tied to the mind which in turn is anchored firmly in theological concepts taught in the Scriptures. "I will sing with the understanding also" (I Cor. 14:15). Music that honors God must not only be heartfelt but also have intellectual validity. "Today's pop music, with notable exceptions, reflects an apathy with regard to the serious issues of modern life. . . . The greatest portion of 'Top 40' music is upbeat, shallow, and suitable for dancing, but not for powerful thought and emotions. And, oddly enough, it is precisely this 'Top 40' style which dominates the entire Christian music industry."[57]

In his interesting work *Will Evangelicalism Survive Its Own Popularity?* Johnston says that "in no area is evangelical faddism more apparent than in our musical preferences and expressions. . . . Musical tastes can be dictated by fads rather than by the deep yearning for true spirituality, . . . and this means that the latest toe-tapping ditty is likely to become our compulsion."[58]

Cultural Adaptation

The notion is prevalent today that, in order to be successful in reaching today's pagans, we must study their culture and seek to adapt the Christian message to it. With utter incredulity, biblical, fundamentalist Christians read some of the statements that are coming from the lips and pens of New Evangelical leaders. It seems that God needs help in converting sinners. We must seek to remove as much of the distinction between the church and the world as possible so as to make the gospel of Christ more palatable. The trouble is that, once that process is begun, the church begins to look more like the world than the world looks like the church. One of the founders of the New Evangelicalism, Carl Henry, in his latter years has made this confession: "While evangelicals seek to penetrate the culture, the culture simultaneously makes disconcerting inroads into evangelical life."[59]

With the advent of the young and worldly evangelicals spoken of earlier in this book, there came a concerted effort to "update" the Christian faith and adapt it to its contemporary surroundings. Quebedeaux admitted this fact some years ago when he said, "The influence of the wider culture on the contemporary evangelical movement has been nothing less than staggering. Marty is correct in declaring that the evangelicals are making more and more compromises with the larger culture."[60]

Modern evangelicals wish to make "the faith" fashionable and acceptable to our contemporaries. We can gain knowledge, say they, from our unsaved neighbors. Understanding of the world "may come as readily from unbelievers as from believers. . . . Non-Christians may enable Christians to see more clearly the implications of the gospel."[61]

In other words, unbelievers, with minds that are totally blinded to spiritual truth and twisted in their perceptions, may be able to instruct Christians as to the nature of this world and its needs. It is strange that the Apostle Paul did not have such insight into the helpfulness of the unsaved. He viewed them rather as "having the understanding darkened, being alienated from the life of God through the ignorance that is in them, because of the blindness of their heart" (Eph. 4:18). Unbelievers cannot correctly analyze the world nor can they correctly tell Christians how to evangelize it since they have absolutely no spiritual understanding. This would certainly negate the advice of one young evangelical who said that we need to develop our theology by "listening to our culture" and by keeping "in scripture."[62] Theology for him has two sources—current culture and Scripture. The historic, and correct position, is that theology is derived solely from the exegesis of Scripture. One does not take the Bible in hand and then keep one ear cocked for the opinions of the worldly. The Bible passes the final judgment on the world, not the world on the Bible.

It ought to be the cause of great concern on the part of Bible-believing Christians that "the rationality of modernity has clearly had a pronounced influence on the world view of Christian Evangelicalism."[63] In what ways does this influence evidence itself? What are some of the characteristics of worldly culture which are being seen in modern Christianity? Kenneth Myers in his book *All God's Children and Blue Suede Shoes* lists some of them.[64]

- Focus on the new
- Reliance on instant accessibility
- Celebration of fame
- Appeal to the sentimental
- Content and form governed by requirements of the market
- Reflection of selfish desires
- Trends towards relativism

All of these can be readily identified in the modern church growth movement, in the ministry of megachurches, in the popular

Contemporary Christian Music, in the preaching of evangelical celebrities, and in the evangelical literature of the day.

While evangelicals, theoretically at least, are committed to the final authority of the Word of God, in practice, through culturally influenced interpretation, they undermine its authority. This observation by Pinnock, while lengthy, is essential in understanding what is happening in current evangelical circles.

> Every generation reads the Bible in dialogue with its own vision and cultural presuppositions and has to come to terms with the world view of its day. . . . Today . . . we are reading the Bible afresh but in the twentieth-century context and finding new insights we had not noticed before. Just as Augustine came to terms with ancient Greek thinking, so we are making peace with the culture of modernity. Influenced by modern culture, we are experiencing reality as something dynamic and historical and are consequently seeing things in the Bible we never saw before. The time is past when we can be naive realists in hermeneutics; who we are influences what we see, and the rich diversity of biblical doctrine means that changes in orientation are always going to be possible, enabling us to communicate in fresh tones to our contemporary hearers.[65]

Study this statement carefully. Pinnock says first of all that our study of the Bible must not be merely an exercise in exegesis, finding out what the Scripture says, but must also be accompanied by input from the culture of the world. This is a totally different approach from that which has been taken historically by fundamentalist interpreters of Scripture. The world is now helping to interpret the Scriptures. This can lead only to spiritual disaster, as it has. We cannot be "realists in hermeneutics," says Pinnock. We cannot simply draw the meaning from Scripture that is there. We must interpret it through the lenses of modernity. In so doing, we shall be "seeing things in the Bible we never saw before." Some evangelicals, embarrassed by the fact that the traditional interpretations of Scripture are out of step with the opinions of our contemporaries, have devised a way of adjusting Scripture to those modern opinions while still maintaining that they are "evangelical." It is a clever hermeneutical manipulation, but one which destroys the inerrancy and authority of Scripture in a manner even more devious than attacks of the "modernists" of old. Modern evangelical hermeneutics, with its subtle twisting of the true meaning of God's Word, is far more dangerous than the more blatant assaults from those who do not claim to be the friends of Scripture.

The Current Search for Novelty

Noted earlier was the list of some characteristics of current evangelicalism. One of these was "the desire for the new." This particular one has become a thorn in the side of many pastors. Members of more traditional, fundamentalist churches have been influenced by the thinking of contemporary evangelicals through personal contact, literature, radio and television, and impressive musical and dramatic extravaganzas. By comparison, the fundamentalist, Bible-preaching church looks rather drab and unexciting, and (heaven forbid!) we must not countenance anything that is not "exciting." Some, particularly among the younger fundamentalist constituency, have become enamored with the approach and style of the New Evangelicals. C. S. Lewis noted that one of the greatest differences between modern men and women and their premodern ancestors is the belief that the new is better than the old.[66] There is a current quest for novelty which has captured much of evangelicalism. Many of the New Evangelical–type churches are much less demanding in their requirements for members, and thus appeal to the "baby boomers" who do not wish to be pressured into strong church commitments. Johnston warns:

> It is open season on "old" church standards. We are prone to ask: What right does my church have to expect me to abide by rules that were established many years ago? Such fossilized standards can only cramp my style, and make me seem old-fashioned to those I am attempting to impress for Christ. Why should I be shackled by such unnecessary weights? Based on this conviction we tend to diminish the number and intensity of the demands made on ourselves and settle in for a less rigorous commitment.[67]

Nowhere in Scripture are we instructed to consult the weathervane of worldly opinion in an effort to create a hearing for the gospel. The world is evil. It is anti-God, a realm of darkness and death. "For all that is in the world, the lust of the flesh, and the lust of the eyes, and the pride of life, is not of the Father, but is of the world" (I John 2:16). James says that "the friendship of the world is enmity with God" (James 4:4). "The world by wisdom knew not God" (I Cor. 1:21), and yet the modern church looks to consult with the wisdom of this world and feels itself the better for having done so. The Lord Jesus Christ is occupied in bringing His people out of the world (John 17:6), not in making them comfortable in it. Believers should be concerned about "overcoming the world" (I John 5:4), not in allowing the world to overcome them.

The Fascination of Psychology

The current evangelical world has become fascinated by psychology. A review of the books of eight major publishers of evangelical literature revealed that 12.3 percent of all titles fell into a category which would be defined as "psychological," that is, the attempt to explain the emotional and psychological needs of man in light of the Bible.[68] This reflects a unique subjectivism in the current evangelical world. It affects the world of the preacher because many of today's evangelicals do not desire doctrinal instruction from the Word of God, but rather homilies or discussions on "how to" meet life's problems and deal with the perplexities of the human soul. "In reaction to the polemics of an earlier generation, they have come to believe that psychological wholeness is a more salutary goal than doctrinal correctness. It is disconcerting to realize that at so many evangelical conferences and retreats, dynamics and small group discussions figure more prominently than scholarly lectures."[69]

As any fundamentalist pastor can testify, there is certainly less interest in the doctrinal and foundational truths of God's Word today than there was years ago. Solid Bible teaching is becoming less popular and is being replaced by pulpit dissertations on psychological themes. It is no doubt true that "psychology is playing a major role in an ongoing and staggering reduction of Christianity."[70]

There is a valid place for scriptural counseling. Personal confrontation and instruction from Scripture are always in order. Paul "exhorted and comforted and charged" the believers at Thessalonica "as a father doth his children" (I Thess. 2:11). He was a biblical counselor. But so much that passes as "Christian counseling" today is anything but that.[71]

Poison in the Pot

New Evangelicalism was born in the minds of evangelical intellectuals. Many of them were professors in various evangelical schools. They touched the lives of thousands of impressionable youth, as do their counterparts today. One after another, institutions of learning that were built and nurtured by old-time fundamentalists began to fall prey to New Evangelical teaching.

How do supposedly evangelical schools drift from their moorings? Primarily, it is through the influence of faculty members. The faculty member has daily touch with the student and—far more than the administrator—has a lasting impact upon him. If one is to maintain a strong, fundamentalist stance, one must hire faculty members who are of that persuasion. But where have many professors at evangelical schools obtained their training? They have graduated from some of the most liberal institutions in the world. While there are isolated examples of great fundamentalists who have come through such institutions unscathed, their numbers are very small. Although a person may not buy into everything to which he is exposed in an institution of higher learning, he will most certainly be greatly influenced by it. "With the proliferation of faculty with the best doctorates in every academic discipline teaching at evangelical seminaries and colleges, it is small wonder that these same institutions have been profoundly influenced by the scholarship produced and taught at the most prestigious secular universities."[72] It is a vicious cycle.

> Many young evangelicals . . . went out into the academic world, and earned their undergraduate and graduate degrees from the finest secular schools. But something happened in the process . . . many of these young evangelicals began to be infiltrated by the anti-Christian world view which dominated the thinking of their colleges and professors. In the process, any distinctively evangelical Christian point of view was accommodated to the secularistic thinking in their discipline and to the surrounding spirit of our age. To make the cycle complete, many of these have now returned to teach at evangelical colleges where what they present in their classes has very little that is distinctively Christian.[73]

Many purportedly Christian colleges and seminaries are far more interested in the prestigious academic credentials of their professors than they are in their spiritual and doctrinal commitment. Hunter, in evaluating his extensive survey of evangelical institutions, remarked, "The focus of education also changed. Perhaps the most concrete measure of this was the shift in the role of the professor. Where previously, orthodoxy (in the correct denomination) had been a major test of an academic's eligibility for a college position, the emphasis was now almost exclusively on the academic's competence and his credentials."[74] One faculty member from an evangelical college said, "Who wants to preserve [religious] dogmatism and [moral] parochialism . . . ? Not me—and not most of my colleagues. We want salient evangelical faith, but since when must this type of religious commitment also include a firm commitment to male-centered households and all the rest of that nasty stuff? What some may call 'contamination' or 'erosion,' I call a 'success.' "[75]

In contrast to this we have the exhortation of Paul who seemed greatly concerned that sound doctrine be passed along from generation to generation. "And the things that thou hast heard of me among many witnesses, the same commit thou to faithful men, who shall be able to teach others also" (II Tim. 2:2). The "things" which Timothy had heard were, of course, the great doctrines of the faith taught to him by Paul. He was to take care to see that these doctrines were preserved intact and delivered to those under his instruction.

Accompanying the deterioration in doctrinal convictions came the deterioration of standards. Whereas almost all Christian colleges used to have rather strict standards of conduct, many, if not most of them, have loosened them considerably. Hunter notes that they even present what standards they do have in a "self-conscious and almost apologetic way."[76] In other words, they seem embarrassed to admit that they have any standards to which students must adhere.

The Charismatic Charisma

The inception of the New Evangelicalism saw an increase in the public acceptance of old-line Pentecostals who formed a large part of the National Association of Evangelicals. Later, as the more recent charismatic movement arose, they have been assimilated into the New Evangelical movement as well and have had a very large influence in it. As a result, changes in evangelicalism have taken place. "The burgeoning charismatic movement also changed the character of much of evangelicalism in important ways. The emphasis shifted . . . toward the experiential aspects of Christianity, a sense of closeness to Jesus through the Spirit dwelling within."[77] We have already commented upon this emphasis, so prominent in evangelicalism. Experience becomes more important, or at least as important, as doctrine.

Evangelical churches, while not always charismatic themselves, cooperate with charismatics and refuse to speak against them. Charles Swindoll, popular author and radio personality, probably sums up the prevailing attitude quite nicely as he tries to defend his concept of grace: "Here's another grace-binding example. I'm not a charismatic. However, I don't feel it is my calling to shoot great volleys of theological artillery at my charismatic brothers and sisters. Who knows how much good they have done and the magnificent ministries many of them have? The church I pastor is not a charismatic church . . . but that does not mean that we break fellowship with individuals who are more of that persuasion or that we take potshots at them."[78]

The question, however, that must be faced, is this: Are the teachings of the charismatics biblical? If the answer is yes, then we should all adopt them. If the answer is no, then we must oppose them. It is not a question of whether charismatics are nice people, or even Christians. At issue is the nature of the truth. Does the Bible teach that there is a gift of tongues operative in the church today, along with other special gifts claimed by many charismatics? If it does not, then faithful Bible teachers cannot sit quietly while such doctrines are spread abroad, infecting large numbers of people. Paul was constantly refuting false doctrine while he ministered to the infant churches. He gave guidance to young pastor Timothy with these words: "In meekness instructing those that oppose themselves; if God peradventure will give them repentance to the acknowledging of the truth" (II Tim. 2:25). The point is that teachers should confront those who err from the truth, seek to correct them, and pray that their eyes will be enlightened and their doctrine changed. If charismatics are wrong in their teaching (and they are), then those who have a better grasp of Scripture should say they are wrong, show them why, and seek to win them to a more biblical position. It is not a mark of Christian grace and love to remain silent in the face of error.

Conclusion

The New Evangelicalism has continued to grow apace. From the small beginnings of the 1950s has come a large and pervasive movement which has captured churches, schools, and parachurch organizations. Those opposing it have been labeled as loveless bigots and narrow-minded obscurantists. But, thank God, there are yet many who have not "bowed the knee" and surrendered to the unbiblical teachings and attitudes of this movement. "Put on the whole armour of God. . . . Stand therefore, having your loins girt about with truth" (Eph. 6:11, 14).

Notes

[1]James D. Hunter, *Evangelicalism: The Coming Generation,* p. 157.

[2]Clark Pinnock, "The Arminian Option," *Christianity Today,* 19 February 1990, p. 15.

[3]Clark Pinnock, "Making Theology Relevant," *Christianity Today,* 29 May 1981, p. 49.

[4]Donald Bloesch, *The Future of Evangelical Christianity,* p. 34.

[5]James D. Hunter, *American Evangelicalism,* p. 132.

[6]Francis Schaeffer, *The Great Evangelical Disaster,* p. 88.

[7]Mark Ellingsen, *The Evangelical Movement,* p. 101.

[8]George Marsden, *Understanding Fundamentalism and Evangelicalism,* p. 64.

[9]Will Durant, *The Story of Philosophy,* p. 116.

[10]"Passing It On: Will Our Kids Recognize Our Faith?" *World,* 11 March 1989, pp. 5-6.

[11]Harold Lindsell, *The Bible in the Balance,* pp. 319-20.

[12]Bloesch, pp. 32-33.

[13]Ibid., p. 118.

[14]Ibid., p. 119.

[15]Ibid., p. 120.

[16]Personal letter to James Hollowood, 15 September 1966.

[17]Richard Quebedeaux, "The Evangelicals: New Trends and New Tension," *Christianity and Crisis,* 23 September 1976, p. 198.

[18]Clark Pinnock, "The Inerrancy Debate Among the Evangelicals," *Theology, News and Notes,* p. 12.

[19]David Hubbard, "What We Believe and Teach," p. 6.

[20]David Hunt and T. A. McMahon, *The Seduction of Christianity*, p. 179.

[21]Francis Schaeffer, p. 60.

[22]Hunter, *Evangelicalism: The Coming Generation*, p. 184.

[23]Stephen Clark, "Modern Approaches to Scriptural Authority," *Christianity Confronts Modernity*, p. 174.

[24]Robert Brow, "Evangelical Megashift," *Christianity Today*, 19 February 1990, p. 12.

[25]Ibid., p. 13.

[26]Ibid., p. 14.

[27]Ibid.

[28]Ibid., p. 12.

[29]Franky Schaeffer, *Bad News for Modern Man*, p. 45.

[30]Bruce Larson, *The Relational Revolution*, p. 32.

[31]Hunter, *American Evangelicalism*, p. 91.

[32]Ibid., p. 88.

[33]Charles Swindoll, *The Grace Awakening*, pp. 227-28.

[34]Carl Henry, "YFC's 'Cheer for Jesus' No Substitute for the Apostolic Creed," *World*, 11 March 1989, p. 7.

[35]Ellingsen, p. 105.

[36]Bloesch, p. 104.

[37]Ibid., pp. 106-7.

[38]Hunter, *Evangelicalism: The Coming Generation*, p. 184.

[39]Hunter, *American Evangelicalism*, pp. 86-87.

[40]Jon Johnston, *Will Evangelicalism Survive Its Own Popularity?*, p. 35.

[41]Ibid., p. 206.

[42] Quebedeaux, pp. 199-200.

[43]Eloise Ressich Fraser, "Evangelical Feminism: The Threat of Its Survival,"*Evangelicalism: Surviving Its Success*, edited by David Fraser, p. 51.

[44]Ibid., p. 52.

[45]Francis Schaeffer, p. 137.

[46]Hunter, *Evangelicalism: The Coming Generation*, p. 103.

[47]Henry, p. 7.

[48]Donald Bloesch, *Crumbling Foundations: Death and Rebirth in an Age of Upheaval*, pp. 21-22.

[49]George Marsden, *Reforming Fundamentalism*, p. 274.

[50]Cited in *This We Believe*, p. 76.

[51]Ian Murray, *David Martyn Lloyd-Jones: The Fight of Faith*, p. 650.

[52]Michael Horton, *Made in America*, p. 155.

[53]Ibid., p. 186.

[54]Robert Pattison, *The Triumph of Vulgarity: Rock Music in the Mirror of Romanticism*, p. 95.

[55]Ibid., p. 186.

[56]Kenneth A. Myers, *All God's Children and Blue Suede Shoes*, p. 150.

[57]Horton, pp. 162-63.

[58]Jon Johnston, p. 115.

[59]Carl Henry, *Confessions of a Theologian*, p. 388.

[60]Richard Quebedeaux, *The Worldly Evangelicals*, p. 10.

[61]Mark Noll and David Wells, editors, *Christian Faith and Practice in the Modern World*, p. 13.

[62]"A Conversation with the Young Evangelicals," *Post-American*, January 1975, p. 10.

[63]Hunter, *American Evangelicalism*, p. 83.

[64]Myers, p. 120.

[65]Clark Pinnock, "From Augustine to Arminius: A Pilgrimage in Theology," *The Grace of God, the Will of Man*, edited by Clark Pinnock.

[66]C. S. Lewis, "De Descriptions Temporum," *They Asked for a Paper: Papers and Addresses*, p. 21.

[67]Johnston, p. 114.

[68]Hunter, p. 94.

[69]Bloesch, *The Future of Evangelical Christianity*, p. 103.

[70]Hunt and McMahon, p. 202.

[71]Space will not be taken here to delineate the problems in this area, but numerous works are available to those interested in pursuing it further. Sample works exposing the errors of some Christian psychologists include John MacArthur, *Our Sufficiency in Christ*; Martin Bobgan, *PsychoHeresy, Prophets of PsychoHeresy I, Prophets of PsychoHeresy II*.

[72]Quebedeaux, pp. 14-15.

[73]Francis Schaeffer, p. 119.

[74]Hunter, *Evangelicalism: The Coming Generation*, p. 167.

[75]Ibid., p. 176.

[76]Ibid., p. 169.

[77]Marsden, *Understanding Fundamentalism and Evangelicalism*, pp. 78-79.
[78]Swindoll, p. 188.

6 **S**alad Bar Sanctuaries

The Concept of "Marketing for Jesus"

One of my wife's favorite restaurant experiences is the trip to the salad bar. She can make a whole meal from the delicacies found there. The wider the selection, the more she enjoys it.

Many contemporary churches have become specialists in operating a spiritual "salad bar." There is something for everyone. If you do not like one offering, you can readily find something else more acceptable to your spiritual palate. Such a "salad bar" approach attracts large numbers of people, but does it build strong churches?

Is the Customer Always Right?

Many modern churches are being built on the concept that one must discover what the marketplace demands and then suit one's ministry to those demands. It is the capitalistic spirit in religious garb. One large church in a midwestern city surveyed its surrounding neighborhoods and asked the residents what kind of church they would prefer to see there. The local residents gave many suggestions, and the church then set about to create a new church patterned after these expressed desires. Those polled, for instance, thought the name "Baptist" was offensive and so the church obligingly dropped the title.

We fail to see any scriptural support for the concept of "church marketing" so widely heralded today. The apostles conducted no surveys of the godless multitudes in Roman cities in order to ascertain what kind of church they might think appropriate. They followed the patterns revealed to them by God, not the opinions uncovered in a neighborhood survey. What do unsaved people know about the proper nature of a church? Nothing! They are spiritually incompetent, blind, and rebellious against God. They do not possess the spiritual ability necessary to assess properly the genuineness of a church. They are dead in trespasses and sins. Dead people do not make very good judgments.

As a matter of fact, the kind of church desired by the average unsaved American may be totally opposite of that described in the New Testament. The unsaved person wants a church that will make him feel good whereas the Lord wants a church that will make him feel the heavy guilt of his sin. The unsaved person likes the jangle of contemporary musical styles whereas the Lord desires music that magnifies the Savior. The unsaved person wants a church that has few standards or requirements whereas the Lord desires a church that calls people to selfless, sacrificial service. The Lord does not invite the unsaved to critique His church because they are "haters of God, . . . proud, . . . [and] without understanding"(Rom. 1:30-31). The will of God as to the organization, methodology, and message of the local church is revealed in the New Testament. These revelations are not subject to adjustment or debate, nor are they open to the correction of those who have no spiritual discernment.

The Aisle to the Salad Bar

The current fad of church marketing was conceived within New Evangelicalism. Many of the leaders of the movement were educated in New Evangelical institutions. Leith Anderson, as an example, is the author of two popular books outlining the church marketing approach. He is a graduate of two leading New Evangelical schools—Conservative Baptist Seminary in Denver and Fuller Theological Seminary.

Principles inherent in New Evangelicalism have appeared also in the church marketing movement where they have been applied specifically to the field of church growth. While some fundamentalists have become enamored with church marketing techniques, it is primarily New Evangelicals that have promoted and practiced them. Some guiding principles that church marketing advocates have inherited from New Evangelicals can be enumerated.

A Disdain for So-Called Negativism

New Evangelicals have shied away from publicly criticizing the theology of other evangelicals. In a similar vein, church marketing advocates advise those who would build successful, growing churches not to criticize the views of fellow believers. As an example, charismatic theology is not challenged by noncharismatics. For this reason charismatics can often feel comfortable in a church whose official doctrinal statement may be noncharismatic.

An Openness to, and Emphasis on, Diversity

New Evangelicals historically have boasted of the great diversity that exists within the general pale of what is called "evangelicalism." They have erected a large umbrella under which persons and churches with many varying convictions can find shelter. This same outlook is found in the church marketing movement. Its spokesmen advise their followers to downplay what they call "denominational distinctives" by which they mean such things as the mode of baptism, church organization, the doctrine of eternal security, and views of the spiritual gifts. There is a call for an emphasis upon more general evangelical truth that is not "divisive."

A Pragmatism in Methodology

With the inception of ecumenical evangelism under the leadership of Billy Graham, a pragmatic spirit developed among evangelicals. "Whatever means result in salvation of souls are acceptable." When critics challenged the ecumenical philosophy, defenders often replied, "But souls are being saved! How can you be against soulwinning?" Thus the disobedient practice of uniting liberals and Bible-believers in the cause of evangelism was fostered. That same general principle now guides those who would tell us how to build our churches. An example is the use of the blaring, raucous sounds of rock music in the sanctuaries of the Lord. The defense of this practice is "It fills our churches and reaches people. Let's do it!"

Truly the aisle leading to the salad-bar sanctuaries comes from the camp of New Evangelicalism. Compromise, a hallmark of New Evangelicalism, is a guiding principle of church marketing.

The Religious Sales Pitch

"A Time to Seek," an article in the secular magazine *Newsweek*, explored the current religious climate and analyzed in particular the factors that are motivating church seekers. The quotations below summarize the general trend of the article.

"Instead of me fitting a religion, I found a religion to fit me."

"In their efforts to accommodate, many clergy have simply airbrushed sin out of their language."

"There's a spirit of putting people over doctrine and denominations."

"The marketplace is now the most widely-used system of evaluation by younger church goers."[1]

One analyst, not a fundamentalist, sounds a warning which should not go unheeded: "We will be tempted to downplay the importance of commitment and obedience. We will be tempted to soften the truth so that a hardened generation will give us a fair hearing. There is a fine line between clever marketing and compromised spirituality."[2] The same writer, in another volume, states, "Often large and growing churches gain numbers by compromising what they believe in order to maintain their growth."[3]

The question is rightly asked, "Does the end justify the means?" Many so-called church growth experts today give the impression that a church should do whatever is necessary in order to attract the throngs. That kind of attitude was roundly condemned by the prophet Isaiah centuries ago as he rebuked the nation Israel: "Woe to them that go down to Egypt for help; and stay [rely] on horses, and trust in chariots, because they are many; and in horsemen, because they are very strong; but they look not unto the Holy One of Israel, neither seek the Lord!" (Isa. 31:1). Israel was rebuked for leaning on the arm of the flesh instead of on the arm of the Lord. The church today is in peril of repeating that error.

Attempting the Impossible

Conferences and seminars on how to build a larger church abound these days, and goodly numbers of pastors frequent them. There are books galore on the subject of church growth. These how-to-do-it presentations give the impression that if the average pastor just applies the suggested methods to his own situation, his church will experience fantastic growth. Unfortunately, it does not prove to be true for the majority. One writer who was himself a successful pastor is nevertheless remarkably candid in his assessment of the current church growth movement: "Evangelical luminaries have done and can do incredible feats. They tell their stunning stories and then deliver an exhortation to the conference, 'You can do it too!' That is, of course, not true for most of the people there. The fact is, the success of a particular pastor is often due to personal charisma, rare leadership, and creative genius that cannot be duplicated by others."[4]

The constant parading of large, numerically successful churches as examples to emulate can be more destructive than helpful. The impression is given that success in the ministry is marked by numerical increase. Pastors whose churches do not evidence remarkable gains feel they have failed.

This author has been preaching God's Word for over fifty years. He has been in hundreds of churches in this country and in others. The average fundamentalist church is not a huge church. The average pastor is not a "super" pastor and never will be. Few men have the abilities required to lead large works with multifaceted ministries. This is no disgrace. Listen carefully to Paul's advice: "For I say, through the grace given unto me, to every man that is among you, not to think of himself more highly than he ought to think; but to think soberly, according as God hath dealt to every man the measure of faith" (Rom. 12:3). The point is that each of God's servants should carefully and realistically evaluate his gifts and be satisfied to minister within the range of those gifts. That one pastor builds a large congregation does not indicate that he is a more spiritual person than the man who has a smaller flock. There are some very spiritual men who have never pastored large congregations.

Go Easy on the Doctrine!

The teaching of sound doctrine has fallen on evil times. Doctrine is considered too heavy and not sufficiently practical to be featured in the preaching of today. Besides, doctrine is divisive and militates against the cry for greater evangelical unity.

One prominent megachurch pastor tells us that we should concentrate on people's needs rather than on what he calls "theocentric" truth:

> For the church to address the unchurched with a theocentric attitude is to write failure in mission. . . . The unconverted will, I submit, take notice when I demonstrate genuine concern about their needs and honestly care about their human hurts.
>
> For decades now we have watched the church in Western Europe and in America decline in power, membership, and

influence. I believe that this decline is the result of our placing theocentric communications above the meeting of deeper emotional and spiritual needs of humanity.[5]

This startling statement demands the restructuring of Christian theology, a move from a God-centered (theocentric) approach to a man-centered (anthropocentric) approach. This is a very serious error that strikes at the very heart of orthodox and biblical theology. Was God's primary purpose in revealing Himself to man to bring honor to Himself or to bring comfort to man? Is the Bible a theocentric book, or is it an anthropocentric book? Although God's revelation in His Son and in His Word brings blessing and comfort to members of the human race, the primary purpose of revelation is not human blessing but divine glory.

The Bottom Line Is Sales

"We must stop reducing the God of the universe to something we can sell to people."[6] To this statement many pastors will say a hearty "Amen." Nevertheless, apparent success has a subtle way of convincing people that the methods employed are perfectly acceptable. But, as one has pointed out, "The nagging question arises: Is our reliance on church growth techniques or on the surprising work of the Holy Spirit?"[7] The whole concept of "church marketing" emphasizes slick sales techniques rather than dependence upon God's power. Forgotten is the principle set forth by the Apostle Paul: "And my speech and my preaching was not with enticing words of man's wisdom, but in demonstration of the Spirit and of power" (I Cor. 2:4). One man, who himself was a very successful pastor, calls attention to the seriousness of the problem that we face today.

> Os Guiness warns that the two most powerful cultural forces that have been accepted uncritically by the church are the managerial and therapeutic movements. The danger is to address church renewal through managerial technique. . . . A "user-friendly" church, if by that we mean catering to the cultural and selfish goals of contemporary fashion, is an unfaithful church. There may be a lot of people in the seats, but have they been confronted with the serious issues raised by the gospel (sin and grace) and the calls to discipleship?[8]

The question every pastor must honestly face is this: Am I building a church that is honoring God and is according to the pattern set forth in His Word? Pastors must be careful how they build. This is the main point of I Corinthians 3:5-17. While this passage is often applied to the lives of individual believers, its main thrust is aimed toward pastors and church planters. Paul is telling us how to build a church, not how to build a life. As a "wise masterbuilder," Paul laid the foundation for the church at Corinth. Others built upon that foundation, and all who labored as leaders of that church (and any other) must eventually give account to God for what they built. "The fire shall try every man's work of what sort it is" (I Cor. 3:13). That is, the quality of the local church will be tested on that great day when all workers and their work are reviewed. It is possible to build a large church that in men's eyes may be eminently successful but that may not pass the final examination of the Lord of the church. The phrase "of what sort it is" emphasizes quality and not quantity. We cannot make the gospel acceptable to a lost world, nor is that task our responsibility. "An analysis of what people like and are accustomed to as a model for what the church should give them tends to minimize the head-on conflict that the gospel always has with the world."[9]

One fails to find the "marketing concept" approved in Scripture. The apostles and early Christians simply preached the gospel in the power of the Spirit and God did the rest. "And the Lord added to the church daily such as should be saved" (Acts 2:47).

The Entertainment Factor

That we live in an entertainment-mad age is self-evident. People want a "thrill a minute." "The early Christians met to worship, pray, fellowship, and be edified—and scattered to evangelize unbelievers. Many today believe that church meetings should entertain unbelievers for the purpose of creating a good experience that will make Christ more palatable to them. . . . They say the church must adopt new methods and innovative programs to grab people on the level where they live."[10]

A perusal of the New Testament will reveal an absence of attention to the entertainment factor in the worship and evangelization ministries of the church. Emphasis is focused upon what people need, not what they want. Michael Horton put his finger on our problem when he wrote,

> By the end of the twentieth century we have become God's demanding little brats. In church, we must be entertained. Our emotions must be charged. . . . We must have the best the world has to offer. . . . We must be offered amusing programs. . . . The preaching must be filled with clever anecdotes and colorful illustrations, with nothing more than passing references to doctrine: "I want to know what this means for me and my daily experience."[11]

An article in the *Wall Street Journal* featured the Second Baptist Church of Houston, Texas, a leading example of a megachurch. Persons attending that church will "catch a Broadway-style show with a religious message. . . . They offer as much in the way of activities and entertainment as they do religion."[12] The church is successful, claims the article, because it has stripped away "old hymns and . . . denominational dogma."[13] In place of these items "teenagers sway and clap at 'Solid Rock.' "[14] The church, we are told, "is primarily designed for a generation unversed in theology, essentially nonsectarian and unsentimental about the old neighborhood church. As churchgoers, they are pragmatic and pressed for time, and they care passionately about . . . dazzling entertainment."[15] The church offers exercise bikes, jacuzzis, and in-house cinema. They once featured a wrestling match with church employees in order to draw a Sunday night crowd.

Multiplying Activities

One of the secrets to building a successful church, we are told, is to have something for everyone. The large megachurches are like their secular counterparts—the megamalls. The more specialty shops one gathers in one place, the more shoppers they are likely to attract. This same principle is being applied to church growth. "Too often the megachurches grow, not because they are superior in their evangelism or better in their preaching or more apt to produce genuine discipleship, but because they have the resources to create special activities appealing to the desires of many different types of groups."[16]

The New Testament gives a rather thorough description of the divinely appointed ministries of a local church. A handy summary of these is found in Acts 2:42: "And they continued stedfastly in the apostles' doctrine and fellowship, and in breaking of bread, and in prayers." New Testament churches were marked by preaching (Acts 20:9), praying (Acts 12:5), singing (Eph. 5:19), giving (I Cor. 16:2), baptizing (I Cor. 1:14-16), observing the Lord's table (I Cor. 11:20-34), and generally encouraging one another (Acts 14:22). The ministry of the church is to be a spiritual ministry. The church is not to become a religious sports and health club, but to be a source of spiritual nourishment and instruction.

Getting on Top of the Heap

One of the religious wonders of modern America is the Crystal Cathedral, pastored by Robert Schuller, a leading guru of the church growth movement. Schuller is a self-confessed disciple of Norman Vincent Peale, the noted New York preacher and religious psychologist. Years ago Schuller went to Southern California and started his ministry. It has grown to tremendous proportions and has become a model for many. What kind of church is it?

> The whole church is program-oriented, the full-time pastoral team functioning as corporate executives. Management principles forged on the anvil of the successful business world are easily transformed into this model. Profit is measured in numerical figures, whether in first-time decisions, membership, or offerings. The team is highly qualified and professional. The undergirding goal is "find the hurt and heal it." This model raises some serious questions as to the extent to which it may have accommodated the Gospel to this expression of the consumer society.[17]

What is motivating so many pastors and churches toward this consumer-driven concept of the ministry? Michael Horton evaluates it this way: "There is something exalting about being a part of something that is respected by society. If we can build larger buildings, have larger gatherings, create larger enterprises, and compete with other mass-produced products, we will be a part of something powerful, something relevant, and the world will have to sit up and take notice of us. . . . That is what was driving the Corinthian believers, too, who had forgotten their roots."[18]

It should be noted that the growth of many churches is not always a result of the evangelization of the lost. "Churches are growing by the rearranging of saints. Evangelicals are simply playing musical churches, moving around to more exciting, larger churches."[19]

Evaluation

What has caused the people of God to get their eyes off of scriptural principles and priorities and to become enamored with fleshly church growth schemes? Os Guiness lists at least four factors which have contributed to the rise of "consumer religion": "(1) The break-up of the monopoly of the old-line denominations upon the religious life of America; (2) the glorification of success; (3) the wide-spread commercialization of our culture; and (4) the effort of Christians to influence the culture."[20] To these factors could be added at least one more: the abandonment of God-centered theology in favor of a pragmatic, man-centered theology. The perception is very common that somehow the sovereign God needs help in accomplishing His purposes on earth. We mortals, therefore, must rush to the rescue of the Almighty, armed with the latest marketing ploys to help deliver the Lord's church from its failures. In an insightful article, Bill Hull asks the question, "Is the Church Growth Movement Really Working?"

> Regretfully, I must answer, "No." And yet, the evangelical church seems to be like a child with a new toy. As churches and pastors expect a more clever gadgetry from the marketing wizards, the latter are encouraged to become increasingly creative until the methods eventually bury the message in obscurity. For that reason, church growth should not be a primer for building effective churches; it has a sociological base, it is data-driven, and it worships at the altar of pragmatism. It esteems that which works above all and defines success in worldly and shortsighted terms. It offers models that cannot be reproduced and leaders who cannot be imitated. The principles of modern business are revered more than doctrine. . . . Yet churches are supposed to be driven by scripture teachings, not by the latest marketing surveys or consumer trends.[21]

It is the nature of the flesh to want recognition and greatness. The sons of Zebedee were supremely concerned about their status in the coming kingdom. "Grant unto us that we may sit, one on thy right hand, and the other on thy left hand, in thy glory" (Mark 10:37). On another occasion the disciples enquired, "Who is the greatest in the kingdom of heaven?" (Matt. 18:1). Their queston sounds hauntingly familiar, similar to the present-day scramble among evangelicals for "bragging rights." The Scriptures give an antidote for this problem: "And seekest thou great things for thyself? seek them not" (Jer. 45:5). How many of God's servants today are spending much thought, time, and energy seeking "great things"? Our goal should be the honor and glory of the blessed Lord. "For I know that the Lord is great" (Ps. 135:5).

Establishing a Comfort Zone

New Evangelical pastors and churches feel a heavy obligation to make all their hearers feel comfortable. They are not to be "threatened" by either the nature of the worship or the message delivered. "Services are often created to minimize discomfort for the unbeliever so that he or she begins to accept Christianity as an affirming influence. People ought to leave church feeling good about themselves, it is said, instead of being called to self-examination, sincere repentance, and faith toward God."[22]

If the Trumpet Gives an Uncertain Sound

New Evangelical thought has had a tremendous impact upon the science of preaching. Down through the centuries God has been pleased to bless the preaching of His Word to the salvation and edification of millions. Preaching, however, has fallen on hard times. This is the age of "sharing" and "interacting." Many do not desire an authoritative pronouncement but rather an "observation" to which other such "observations" can be compared. It is a day of humanism in preaching.

Let's Be Positive

To New Evangelicals the cardinal sin is negative preaching. Repeatedly we are told by those who would tell us how to build large churches that we are to be "affirmative" rather than "prophetic" in our preaching. Basically one is affirmative when his listeners have a positive feeling about themselves rather than a negative one. So-called prophetic preaching is that kind of preaching which makes the hearer feel uncomfortable. Leith Anderson declares that "preaching has changed from the days when the parishioners at the door said, 'Thanks, pastor. You really stepped on our toes today, and I loved it.'"[23] The most important question, however, is this: What kind of preaching is approved by God? What guidelines for preaching are set forth in God's Word?

Observers of the current religious scene have noted that moderns do not desire the same type of preaching that their forefathers did. One observer believes we should abandon the superchurches as models for the average church and notes that such churches major "in 'positive preaching' (confrontational preaching has not found a spot on most church growth lists I've seen)."[24] In the biography of Robert Schuller, a current model for the church growth movement, the author states that Schuller learned from Norman Vincent Peale, the liberal Manhattan pastor, that we should treat people positively. We should avoid making them feel guilty but rather make them feel good about themselves.[25] If a preacher can make enough people feel good about themselves, he can draw quite a crowd. People like to be made to feel good, to feel they have the inner potential to "make it work," to succeed in life. No wonder that contemporary "ear ticklers" can attract such huge audiences.

Matzat makes a strong plea for a return to biblical preaching, to an emphasis upon sin and grace.

> And yet, the very approach I am suggesting, which has been characteristic of evangelical preaching and teaching for centuries, and lies at the very heart of the Biblical revelation, is anathema in many evangelical circles today. Roy Anderson, who teaches a course on the integration of self-esteem and theology at Fuller Theological Seminary in Pasadena, California, complains about the psychological battering of the cross. . . . There is no doubt that the cross does inflict upon us a "psychological battering." Theologically, we have considered that to be part of the process leading to repentance.[26]

What a telling remark is the following: "People today hunger not for personal salvation . . . but for the feeling, the momentary illusion of personal well-being, health, and psychic security."[27] It is no doubt true, but should we aim in our preaching to satisfy these desires of the flesh? Experienced pastors have often heard the complaint, "But, pastor, you are not meeting my needs." One has correctly observed that the "focus is on oneself rather than on Christ."[28] Another has noted, "By preaching to 'felt needs' we are often preaching to selfish and idolatrous cravings."[29] If preachers give in to these current notions, they will be giving people what they want to hear rather than what God wants them to hear. There is a big difference.

Psychology and the Pulpit

As previously noted, evangelical Christians have become enamored with psychology. This fascination has definitely had its effect upon preaching. People are more interested in having their feelings explored and diagnosed than they are in hearing objective truth from the Scriptures. "We are living in an age where the focus of ministry is upon counseling and group manipulation rather than upon preaching. Expertise in psychology and in church management are deemed more important than immersion in the Word of God."[30]

Is the preacher to be mainly a pulpit psychologist, applying "spiritual Band-Aids" to the emotional hurts of his hearers, or is he to be a proclaimer of the rich and varied truths of the Word of God? Much preaching today, particularly in those churches thought to be models of success, is centered on psychological themes—meeting a person's emotional needs, helping individuals achieve self-esteem, and solving their personal and interpersonal problems. The Bible becomes a textbook in psychology. "Personality theory, psychopathology, health, and therapeutic change have replaced Biblical anthropology, sin, grace, holiness, and sanctification. Psychology's culture, social, and pragmatic authority proved too strong. Biblical truth seemed insufficiently applicable."[31]

How sad for one to think that biblical truth is inapplicable today! The Word of God was written to meet the needs of men, but, more important, to reveal the thoughts of God and to direct man away from himself and toward the Lord. The emphasis today is upon "my needs" rather than upon God's person. Preachers have, in response, been turning away from the exposition of biblical truth and have scurried about to locate verses and passages that would "meet needs." Those who do not "meet needs" may be in danger of losing their jobs!

Let's Share Ideas

Some people's concept of Bible study is to gather a group together, have them open their Bibles, and then go around the circle having each share "what this passage means to me." Under most circumstances this practice results merely in an accumulation of ignorance. The first question one must ask is: "What does the passage mean?" not "What does it mean *to me?*" In order to answer that question, one must have spiritual discernment and some knowledge of the principles of biblical interpretation. However, most unfortunately, many persons are not nearly as interested in what God said as they are in finding answers to their problems. Much preaching today is infected with this subjective and selfish approach to the examination of God's revelation. Leith Anderson notes that old-style preaching used to "tell people what to do." But times have changed. "Modern Americans don't want their politicians, doctors, or pastors telling them what to do. . . . Today's speaker is more of a 'communicator' than a 'preacher.' The older-style preaching was marked by such words as 'ought,' and 'should' and 'must.' "[32] Such language is to be avoided by those who would build large and successful churches.

The great British expositor, Martyn Lloyd-Jones, some years ago lamented certain influences which were undermining the character and authenticity of modern preaching. One of these was the change from "preaching to sharing. . . . Worship was 'liberated.' "[33] When the approach of "sharing" is adopted, one's attention immediately is diverted from God's revelation to man's perception.

Current expectations for preachers have caused many a man of God to rethink his approach. Should I give in to the demands of the people, forsake the expository approach, and deliver "sermonettes" to "Christianettes"? These are hard questions facing pastors today.

> The world wants religion to answer "practical" questions about relationships, child-rearing, self-image, lifestyle, "how to do" this or that. God must not interrupt! He must never get in the way.
>
> Religion must never tell a person what he or she must believe or do. It must simply help the world solve its practical problems.[34]

For centuries Christians have found the answers to life's deepest problems in the teaching of Scripture. But these answers have been discovered as applications of the great doctrinal truths about God and His works. The great preachers of the past have not gone to the Scriptures with the primary aim of meeting human need but of finding and declaring the mind and purpose of God. In so doing, they have met human needs.

Please Don't Make Me Think!

Modern Americans have been raised on a steady diet of entertainment. Television has affected our culture to a very large extent. Preachers are now confronted every Sunday with members who have spent hours that week in viewing the very latest in entertainment. Television has made the general public very entertainment conscious. It has definitely had an adverse impact upon people's ability (and desire) to think and to follow reasoned arguments. Since preaching is based upon reasoning and the orderly marshaling of ideas, it becomes difficult for many moderns to follow an exposition of the Bible. One has rightly observed of television:

> Its form of communication (and form of knowing) encourages the aversion to abstraction, analysis, and reflection that characterizes our culture at all levels. Thinking is often hard work.
>
> Television's surfeit of instant entertainment not only provides relief from such hard work, it offers an attractive, alternative, "way of knowing" (as does rock 'n' roll) that makes reasoning seem anachronistic, narrow, and unnecessary.[35]

In an interesting examination of the differences between "Pre-Boomers," "Baby Boomers," and "Baby Busters," Gary McIntosh notes that "while expository sermons used to be thought of as the order of the day, baby boomers and baby busters now want 'how to' sermons and 'issue-oriented' sermons."[36] In light of this trend, however, the preacher must ask, "Is genuine, acceptable preaching a declaration of what God wants man to hear or of what man wants God to say?" Historically, preaching has been viewed as the art of communicating to men, in language understandable to them, the timeless truths from the Bible about God and His works. The starting point for preaching has been God and not man. This is not to say that true biblical preaching is in any way impractical. In such preaching, however, the preacher begins with an exposition of what God says, and then makes application to man's personal needs. The Bible was not written merely to satisfy man's needs and to give him answers to his everyday problems. It was written to show forth the majesty of God and to trace God's purposes for the created universe, angels, earth, Israel, and the church. That one does not receive a "blessing" from some portion of Scripture when it is expounded, does not necessarily mean that the exposition was ill-chosen or worthless. To judge preaching by its personal impact alone is to view it from a selfish perspective. "In fact, there is a trend in contemporary evangelicalism away from expository, doctrinal preaching and a movement toward an experience-centered, pragmatic, shallow, topical approach in the pulpit. . . . Churchgoers are seen as consumers who have to be sold something they like."[37]

One of the chief purveyors of the "new approach" in preaching is Leith Anderson, pastor of a megachurch in the Twin Cities. His two books *Dying for Change* and *A Church for the 21st Century* have made a great impact upon the thinking of many young preachers and are considered to be among the leading statements of the philosophy of church growth promoted by New Evangelicals. Because of Anderson's prominence in this field, we pause to consider what he has said about preaching and matters that relate directly to preaching.

> The old paradigm taught that if you have the right teaching, you will experience God. The new paradigm says that if you experience God, you will have the right teaching. This may be disturbing for some who assume that propositional truth must always precede and dictate religious experience. That mindset is a product of systematic theology and has much to contribute. . . . However, biblical theology looks to the Bible for a pattern of experience followed by proposition. The experience of the Exodus from Egypt preceded the recording of the Exodus in the Bible.[38]

This alarming statement graphically illustrates the shift of emphasis which has taken place in the modern church. Experience is magnified over knowledge and actually becomes the judge of knowledge. Invalid is the argument that the exodus supports the theory that the experience of God precedes the knowledge of God. God clearly imparted much knowledge about Himself to Moses and the children of Israel *prior to His deliverance of them from the land of Egypt.* God appeared to Moses, spoke to Moses, and instructed him that He would bring His people out of Egypt and into the Promised Land (Exod. 6:1-8). The various plagues upon the land of Egypt were revelatory in nature (Exod. 7-11) and prepared the people for the exodus experience. Of course the book of Exodus was written after the events themselves took place, but this fact in no way demonstrates the idea that revelation follows experience. The revelation to ancient Israel at this time in their history was through Moses, was direct and immediate, and was not delivered by inscripturation. Explicit instructions were given as to how the Israelites were to leave the land of Egypt. These instructions were preceded by such phrases as "the Lord said" (Exod. 11:1) and "the Lord spake" (Exod. 12:1) These phrases indicate divine revelation, such revelation preceding the actual events of the exodus and providing the basis upon which Moses acted as he led the Israelites from captivity.

According to Anderson's paradigm, one's experience with God is the standard by which one judges the correctness of teaching. This is completely contrary to what the Scriptures teach and also to the historic position of orthodox Christians. In the matter of personal salvation, the unbeliever hears a message (propositional truth) and then experiences salvation. "Believe on the Lord Jesus Christ [propositional truth], and thou shalt be saved [the experience of regeneration]" (Acts 16:31). The same order is given in Romans 6:17-18 where Paul rejoices that his readers had "obeyed from the heart that form of doctrine which was delivered you." Following their acceptance of this propositional truth, they then experienced freedom from the tyranny of sin (v. 18).

As we have already mentioned in other contexts, one of the chief errors of New Evangelicals is their tendency to overemphasize experience to the neglect of sound teaching. The charismatics have led the way in developing this mindset and have influenced evangelicalism in general. This is the reason so-called Christian rock is popular. People want to "feel" something rather than "learn" something. It also explains the current fascination with so-called Christian psychology. Again, people want to "feel good about themselves" but are far less interested in digesting any systematic diet of Scripture.

"I Don't Like Broccoli."

George Bush, when president of the United States, created a stir among broccoli growers, and gave support to many small children, when he announced publicly that he did not care for broccoli. Many believers have the same aversion to sound doctrine. Any attempt to broach doctrinal issues is to many contemporary believers a bore and a bother. Here Leith Anderson (and others of his persuasion) encourage this attitude. Anderson cites various historic differences within the church: Arminianism vs. Calvinism; infant vs. adult

143

baptism; the validity of charismatic gifts; the form of church government; and Reformed vs. dispensational theology. He points out that "there is a fast-growing church population that considers most of these distinctives to be irrelevant. They don't really care about these differences, and they demonstrate their attitudes by easily moving from church to church with differing ideologies."[39] Any experienced pastor could certainly confirm the fact that many modern believers seem to have no care for doctrinal differences. One may visit the retirement communities in Florida or Arizona and discover numbers of former members of sound, fundamentalist churches in the North who now attend the most rank New Evangelical congregations and do not seem to realize that there is anything amiss. Anderson continues to shock us as he describes the average churchgoer today and encourages us to cater to their whims. "The differences between Catholicism and Protestantism don't matter very much, if at all, compared to the importance of a Sunday School they and their children like. Sometimes they say, 'When the kids are grown we'll think about going back to the Catholic Church' "[40] Real convictions, these! The greater tragedy is that these New Evangelical preachers and congregations will not tell them what is wrong with the Catholic church. That would be too negative, confrontational, and divisive. "For if the trumpet give an uncertain sound, who shall prepare himself to the battle?" (I Cor. 14:8). There are far too many "uncertain sounds" in the pulpits of the land.

Broad parameters of fellowship and loose doctrinal convictions are bound to affect the preaching of a pastor. One pastor describes a program his church provides to assist other churches in learning how to grow. "Half a dozen churches participate at one time—often including charismatic and non-charismatic, mainline and independent, young and old. No attempt is made to change doctrinal or denominational distinctives. . . . The day is fast disappearing when people choose churches because of the name of the denomination, the mode of baptism, or the system of theology."[41]

But questions must be asked. Does the Bible teach both charismatic doctrine and noncharismatic doctrine? Can both baptismal regeneration and salvation by faith alone be supported from the Scriptures? If someone is teaching error, should a pastor or teacher rebuke it and correct it? These serious questions define the very nature of the ministry. John Stott is absolutely right when he says that "theology is far more important than methodology" [42] and that preaching must have a solid theological basis.

Don't Be So Dogmatic.

Strong convictions are not in fashion these days, particularly in the religious world. "Live and let live" is the motto. This mindset has already been noted in previous discussions. It certainly is affecting the attitudes of many toward the preaching ministry. Barna observes, "By 2000, Americans will be even less interested in absolutes, preferring those perspectives which allow for relative values to gain credence. Casting issues in a black-and-white mode will disgust many people."[43] No doubt this observation contains some truth, but should God's messengers be intimidated by this trend and mute their message from God? Should the preacher refrain from seeking to discover the clear meaning of the scriptural text for fear that some will disagree with him? Charles Spurgeon was criticized severely in his day for his public and repeated defense of great doctrines of the faith and yet God mightily blessed his ministry. There was no effort on the part of the Apostle Paul to be less dogmatic. "As we said before, so say I now again, if any man preach any other gospel unto you than that ye have received, let him be accursed" (Gal. 1:9). Paul would not have made a good New Evangelical. He was far too abrasive in his dogmatism.

Hanging Loose

In earlier days preachers emphasized to people the importance of membership in a local congregation. In contrast, one current author sees church membership as meaningless. "It is a concept born in another era. In America today, with the values of people changing rapidly and significantly, long-term loyalty and commitment are passé concepts. There are growing numbers of people who, even if they attend a church regularly, and are active participants in the ministry of the Body, refuse to join the church."[44]

Why would this be true? Why would people not wish to affiliate themselves with a local congregation? "Church membership has negative connotations today. People perceive it to be restrictive and to provide few benefits. . . . In other words, the average adult thinks that belonging to a church is good for other people but represents unnecessary bondage and baggage for himself."[45]

145

Another notes that many wish to attend a church but do not wish to join. "They view local churches more as networks than formal organizations."[46] In other words, they want to "network" (fellowship and make friends) without making any commitment to the position and ministry of the church itself. The old-fashioned (and we believe, biblical) concept of a church covenant is obsolete. The church covenant is a solemn agreement between the members of the congregation, before the Lord, that they will seek to live godly lives, attend and support the church, and so on. Nowadays the local church is viewed as a convenience for the benefit of people. This is evident in the quotation given previously indicating that people view church membership as "providing few benefits." It is another indication of the inherent selfishness of the age in which we live. "I will support something to the extent that I think it benefits me and my family. If these benefits are not as great as I think they should be, I will go elsewhere." One is reminded of Paul's lament, "For all seek their own, not the things which are Jesus Christ's" (Phil. 2:21).

Contrary to the notions of some, church membership is both biblical and important. The first church was formed by the bonding together of converts who "continued stedfastly in the apostles' doctrine and fellowship, and in breaking of bread, and in prayers" (Acts 2:42). The language employed indicates a high degree of commitment to the local body. It is vital that believers be accountable to a local church, a vital part of a functioning body, and not merely observers who float in and out at will. Many churches make the mistake of allowing non-members to participate in the ministry of the church without making any definite commitment to its doctrinal position or standards. They view this as a display of Christian love and acceptance, but, in reality, they are weakening the position of their church and making church membership virtually meaningless.

True churches that have a desire to be biblical should have some standards for their members. While some today decry this as "legalism," it is both scriptural and wise. A. W. Tozer, a leader years ago in the denomination known as the Christian and Missionary Alliance, had great spiritual discernment and the courage to declare the unpopular. Would that those who are following in his train today had the same spiritual fortitude! He wrote,

Evangelical Christianity is fast becoming the religion of the bourgeois. The well-to-do, the upper-middle classes, the politically prominent, are accepting our religion by the thousands . . . to the uncontrollable glee of our religious leaders who seem completely blind to the fact that the vast majority of these new patrons of the Lord of glory have not altered their moral habits in the slightest nor given any evidence of true conversion that would have been accepted by the saintly fathers who built the churches.[47]

Scriptural Guidelines for Preaching

We have seen that the New Evangelical philosophy has influenced preaching in the following ways:

1. An overemphasis on the positive aspects of preaching while neglecting its warning aspects.

2. An occupation with psychology.

3. A replacement of authoritative pronouncement with the concept of "sharing" ideas.

4. "Issues-oriented" preaching rather than reasoned exposition.

5. Preaching to what people want rather than what they need.

6. A retreat from what is viewed as "dogmatism."

In light of this emphasis which has developed within New Evangelical circles there is an urgent need to review the biblical guidelines for preaching. Preaching is the act of communicating God's Word to men. Certainly within the pages of the Bible we should be able to discover some divine principles for this great task.

Our Preaching Source—Inerrant Scripture

Much of the weakness in today's preaching can be traced back to a weak view of the inspiration and authority of Scripture. While there are differences among New Evangelicals over this question, there has been a noticeable drift to weaker positions on inspiration in recent years. Francis Schaeffer in his probing book *The Great Evangelical Disaster* sounds the warning: "But what is happening in evangelicalism today? Is there the same commitment to God's absolutes which the early church had? Sadly we must say that this commitment is not there. . . . Evangelicalism is not unitedly standing for a strong view of Scripture. We must say with sadness that in some places seminaries, institutions, and individuals who are known as evangelicals no longer hold to a full view of Scripture."[48]

If one does not hold to the full inspiration of Scripture, it will certainly affect his preaching. If a preacher has questions concerning the complete inspiration of a given passage, he will not be able to expound it with authority. The command to "preach the word" (II Tim. 4:2) is preceded by the classic passage on inspiration. "All scripture is given by inspiration of God" (II Tim. 3:16), and upon the basis of that truth we preach. Commitment to the complete inerrancy of the Bible gives the preacher confidence and helps him preach with power and authority.

Expository Preaching

As we have already seen, there is a move on the part of some evangelical leaders to discount the value of expository preaching and to emphasize "issues" preaching. A correct and complete definition of expository preaching is not easy to come by, as can be verified by an examination of various texts on the subject. However, for our purposes here we can say that expository preaching is that style of preaching that endeavors to exegete, explain, and apply a passage or passages of Scripture, taking into consideration the argument of the writer, the grammatical construction, the historical setting, and the theological implications. The expositor's first concern is: "What does the passage say?" His next concern is "What does the passage mean?" Answering these questions involves an application of the laws of hermeneutics. His final concern is "What does the passage mean to me?" This is application. Our first concern, however, should be to discover what God intended to say in the passage, not what we would like the passage to say.

While no formal definitions of expository preaching exist in Scripture, there is an excellent summary of some of its ingredients found in Nehemiah 8:8—"So they read in the book of the law of God distinctly, and gave the sense, and caused them to understand the reading." In a word, the teachers of Israel took passages of Scripture, moved from verse to verse, and explained the meaning of the verses in their context. They were, in fact, expounding the Scriptures. Expository preaching has a number of advantages:

1. It honors the doctrine of biblical inspiration, holding the preacher to the text and emphasizing to the congregation the sacredness of the written Word.
2. It keeps the preacher from unsupported flights of fancy.

3. It enables the preacher to cover many different areas of divine truth over a period of time rather than concentrating on favorite subjects and matters of particular interest.

4. Consistently practiced by a pastor over a long period of time, it provides a congregation with a biblical education that will produce spiritual maturity and depth of Christian living.

My Opinion or God's Directive?

Historically, biblical Christians have held that the objective truths of the written Scriptures supersede and authoritatively interpret all professed Christian experience. But this concept has been challenged by some New Evangelicals.

> Biblical authority has been undermined by the rise of spiritualism, where the appeal is to the inner light or the voice of the Spirit rather than to the written Word of God. In these circles it is assumed that there is a discontinuity between what the Spirit said in biblical times and what he says today. It is also contended that the Spirit is speaking through the social sciences and politics, and this means that the Bible is therefore interpreted in the new light that comes to us from the social sciences.[49]

While not all New Evangelicals would see it the same way, many have been influenced toward a more subjective approach to biblical interpretation. The charismatic movement has aided this with their appeal to extrabiblical "revelations."

The preaching described in the Bible is authoritative. "For our gospel came not unto you in word only, but also in power, and in the Holy Ghost, and in much assurance" (I Thess. 1:5). The words "in much assurance" could be rendered "with deep conviction," referring to the strongly held convictions of the preacher, not the hearer. Our blessed Lord "taught them as one having authority, and not as the scribes" (Matt. 7:29). The rabbinical teachers of the day quoted one another, and often were indefinite as to exactly what the Scriptures taught; but Jesus was not so. Those who would preach like Jesus must be definite, clear, decisive, and settled. Christ's authority, of course, resided in Himself. Our authority resides in the Holy Scriptures. One of the words for the gospel preacher in the New Testament is *kerux*. It is used for instance in II Timothy 1:11 where Paul declares he was appointed a "preacher." A preacher is a "herald," "a messenger vested with public authority, who conveyed the official message of kings, magistrates, princes, military commanders, or who gave a public summons or demand" (*Thayer's Lexicon*). A herald was not consulting with the populace to ascertain what message they would like to hear. He was going forth with confidence, proclaiming without change the message he had been given whether people wished to hear it or not. The modern world needs to hear messengers who come from the throne of the Almighty with the timeless message of good news.

Being Against Something

A mature Christian woman in a congregation I served as pastor came to me on one occasion and said, "I'm so glad I have a pastor who is against some things and isn't afraid to say so publicly." Not all Christians have been carried away with the disease of "positivism" that seems to have captured so much of modern Christendom. There are discerning saints who see through this current façade and grasp the heart of the issue.

God is opposed to preachers who "speak a vision of their own heart, and not out of the mouth of the Lord" (Jer. 23:16). They are "prophets of the deceit of their own heart" (Jer. 23:26). Modern New Evangelical preachers would not use such harsh language to describe those who are teaching error, but God's ancient prophet did. Isaiah said of his people Israel, "Ah sinful nation, a people laden with iniquity, a seed of evildoers, children that are corrupters: they have forsaken the Lord, they have provoked the Holy One of Israel unto anger, they are gone away backward" (Isa. 1:4). It is this type of preaching which is not popular today and which New Evangelicals refer to as "prophetic" preaching. Their cry is for "affirmative" rather than "prophetic" preaching. But what kind of preaching does God want, and what kind of preaching is exemplified in Scripture? The greatest preacher who ever walked this earth, the Lord Jesus Christ, uttered scathing denunciations of the Pharisees, often repeating the phrase "Woe unto you, scribes and Pharisees, hypocrites!" (Matt. 23:13, e.g.). Such outspokenness would be an embarrassment to the New Evangelicals of our day even though the words were uttered by the kindest and most loving person this world has ever seen.

We are not appealing here for uncouth, vitriolic, or deliberately abrasive preaching. Some preachers, in their zeal to "take a stand," become mean and nasty in their pulpit ministry, harp on petty issues, and fail to feed the flock of God. Our task is to be "speaking the truth in love" (Eph. 4:15). Only a Spirit-controlled believer can display this balance in his life.

The Diet of Doctrine

One of the preacher's main responsibilities is to teach sound doctrine. Paul describes the work of the preacher in this way: "Holding fast the faithful word as he hath been taught, that he may be able by sound doctrine both to exhort and to convince the gainsayers" (Titus 1:9). The verse tells us that the man of God must be (1) loyal to Scripture, (2) knowledgeable in theology, (3) a teacher of doctrine, and (4) an outspoken opponent of false teaching. Regrettably, many of these elements are lacking in the contemporary pulpit. For this reason there is many a saint who is shrivelled, weak, and blown about by various "winds."

In the process of preaching the Word, God's messengers are to "exhort with all longsuffering and doctrine" (II Tim. 4:2). How does God judge whether a pastor is a good pastor? Paul says that a "good minister of Jesus Christ" will be "nourished up in the words of faith and of good doctrine" (I Tim. 4:6). Before mentioning other characteristics of his ministry, Paul reminds Timothy that he has "fully known" Paul's "doctrine" (II Tim. 3:10). Paul puts that first in the list as if to say, "My doctrine is very important and I want everyone to know exactly what it is."

The modern concept of what constitutes a good preacher and good preaching is often in conflict with the pattern set forth in the Bible. Unsaved persons and carnal Christians are not reliable guides when seeking to develop a philosophy of preaching. The only accurate and authoritative "guide to preaching" is the Word of God itself.

Notes

[1]*Newsweek,* "A Time to Seek," 17 December 1990.

[2]George Barna, *The Frog in the Kettle,* p. 123.

[3]George Barna, *User Friendly Churches,* p. 64.

[4]Bill Hull, "Is the Church Growth Movement Really Working?" *Power Religion,* p. 146.

[5]Robert Schuller, *Self-Esteem: The New Reformation,* p. 12.

[6]Gregory Lewis, *Is God For Sale?* p. 16.

[7]Donald Bloesch, *The Future of Evangelical Christianity,* p. 100.

[8]Hull, p. 144.

[9]Tom Nettles, "A Better Way: Church Growth Through Revival and Reformation," *Power Religion,* p. 183.

[10]John MacArthur, *Our Sufficiency in Christ,* p. 31.

[11]Michael Scott Horton, *Made in America,* pp. 87-88.

[12]"Mighty Fortresses: Megachurches Strive to Be All Things to All Parishioners," *Wall Street Journal,* 13 May 1991.

[13]Ibid.

[14]Ibid.

[15]Ibid.

[16]Ibid.

[17]Peter Savage, "The Church and Evangelism" in *The New Face of Evangelism,* edited by C. René Padilla, p. 108.

[18]Michael Scott Horton, "The Subject of Contemporary Relevance," *Power Religion,* p. 333.

[19]Hull, p. 143.

[20]Os Guiness, *The Gravedigger File,* pp. 130-33.

[21]Hull, pp. 141-42.

[22]Don Matzat, "A Better Way: Christ Is My Worth," *Power Religion,* p. 253.

[23]Leith Anderson, *A Church for the 21st Century,* p. 201.

[24]Hull, p. 174.

[25]James Penner, *Goliath: The Life of Robert Schuller.*

[26]Matzat, p. 26.

[27]Christopher Lasch, *The Culture of Narcissim,* p. 31.

[28]Edward Welch, "Codependency and the Cult of the Self," *Power Religion,* p. 226.

[29]Horton, p. 331.

[30]Bloesch, p. 147.

[31]David Powlinson, "Integration or Inundation?" *Power Religion,* p. 199.

[32]Anderson, p. 209.

[33]Ian Murray, *David Martyn Lloyd-Jones: The Fight of Faith,* p. 667.

[34]Horton, p. 342.

[35]Kenneth Myers, *All God's Children and Blue Suede Shoes,* p. 171.

[36]Gary McIntosh, "What's in a Name?" *The McIntosh Church Growth Network,* vol. 3, no. 5 (May 1991), p. 2.

[37]MacArthur, pp. 133-34.

[38]Anderson, p. 21.

[39]Ibid., p. 32.

[40]Ibid.

[41]Ibid., pp. 32-33.

[42]John R.W. Stott, "Biblical Preaching Is Expository Preaching," *Evangelical Roots,* edited by Kenneth Kantzer, p. 160.

[43]Barna, *The Frog in the Kettle,* p. 121.

[44]Barna, *User Friendly Churches,* pp. 23-24.

[45]Barna, *The Frog in the Kettle,* p. 133.

[46]Anderson, pp. 48-49.

[47]Cited in David Fant, *A.W. Tozer: A Twentieth Century Prophet,* p. 50.

[48]Francis Schaeffer, *The Great Evangelical Disaster,* p. 49.

[49]Donald Bloesch, "The Challenge Facing the Churches," *Christianity Confronts Modernity,* p. 208.

7 Gray Hairs Are Here and There

The Subtle Drift Toward the New Evangelicalism

Those television ads are alluring! Aimed as they are toward the millions whose hair is graying, they boldly announce—"Gradually the gray just disappears. You wash the gray right out." For the price of a few bottles of the right mixture, one can supposedly retrieve his youthful look again.

The ancient prophet Hosea was concerned about gray hair also, but for a different reason. In a brokenhearted lament over his beloved nation, Israel, he wrote: "Strangers have devoured his strength, and he knoweth it not: yea, gray hairs are here and there upon him, yet he knoweth not" (Hos. 7:9). Gray hairs are a mark of aging, of deteriorating strength, and, in the spiritual sense employed by Hosea, of a loss of spiritual vitality. The saddest note in this lament was the fact that the nation did not realize it was losing its spiritual moorings.

All over America and the world at this hour there are churches that are drifting into New Evangelicalism without the remotest knowledge that they are doing so. They are being carried along with the shifting winds of compromise and have long since departed from the solid biblical position established by their predecessors. Young pastors, many without firm doctrinal underpinnings, have led their churches to believe that in order to reach the masses they must abandon the strict biblical principles of yore and embrace more fluid and attractive positions. They have changed, but they do not realize that they have changed. Many saints, firmly indoctrinated by former pastors in clear and uncompromising positions, are now bewildered and drifting from church to church seeking some stability.

The Appeal of New Evangelicalism to the Fundamentalist

Many contemporary fundamentalists are being wooed by the siren call of New Evangelicalism. It seems especially compelling to younger men (though not exclusively so). Born in a different generation and without personal involvement in the battles against the early forms of New Evangelicalism, some are impatient with the fray, do not see the relevance of the conflict, and are inclined to adopt the attitude "a plague on both your houses." What is there about the New Evangelicalism that seems to attract some from within the fundamentalist camp?

A Lessening of Tensions

Establishing and maintaining a strong fundamentalist stand in this present society is very wearing emotionally, physically, and spiritually. One must constantly be on the alert and is consigned to be forever in a battle. This of course is perfectly in order with what Scripture teaches. Against the hosts of hell we are to "wrestle" and we are to "stand" (Eph. 6:11-14). We have responded to the bugle that never blows retreat. We have sworn eternal enmity against the forces of unrighteousness; thus there is no discharge from the war in which we are engaged. The battle is tough. It becomes particularly distasteful when one must oppose brethren in the Lord. Many cannot take the pressure. It is better, they think, to have a less confining position so that one will not have quite as many people against which to contend. The New Evangelical position seems to offer some relief from certain aspects of conflict. It thus becomes a very tempting position to consider. The psalmist must have foreseen the twentieth century when he wrote, "The children of Ephraim, being armed, and carrying bows, turned back in the day of battle" (Ps. 78:9). How cowardly! To turn from the field of conflict when the lives of others and the future of their nation depended upon their courage in battle!

> Nor think the battle won,
>   nor lay thine armor down.
> The fight of faith will not be done
>   till thou hast won the crown.

With what joy and satisfaction could the apostle Paul write at the end of his earthly ministry: "I have fought a good fight" (II Tim. 4:7). He had battles with the Judaizers, battles with the chief priests and Jewish leaders, battles with the priests of paganism, battles with some church leaders, and battles with many who opposed and sought to subvert his ministry. He did not shirk the conflicts, though they wore upon his soul and no doubt brought him to an earlier grave. We dare not choose the easier path but must follow our Lord who carried his cross of shame to Golgotha.

A Wider Working Relationship

Some fundamentalists have become disturbed by the fact that their circle of fellowship is considerably narrowed due to their strict position. They meet winsome, pleasant personalities from the New Evangelical camp and wonder why they cannot fellowship and work with them even though there may be important theological and methodological differences. New Evangelicals, in their fellowships, cross many denominational and theological lines and this "freedom of movement" seems attractive to some fundamentalists. A noted itinerant Bible teacher was asked by a friend of mine why it was he never spoke on the issues of separation or the New Evangelicalism in the large conferences he addressed. The man replied, "It closes too many doors." New Evangelicals have many doors of opportunity opened to them simply because they do not address publicly "sticky" issues that are likely to cause these doors to close. Loyalty to the truth can put one in a very lonely position. Paul, disturbed in his soul, said, "All men forsook me" (II Tim. 4:16). How alone he must have felt; yet the Lord stood with him!

A Greater Attractiveness to the Masses

New Evangelicals have bombarded fundamentalists with the accusation that the fundamentalist position is too narrow and that it repels rather than attracts the people of the world. Those who are paraded before us as the role models of success in church growth are almost all of the New Evangelical persuasion. It is no wonder that young fundamentalists question whether they too should adopt the New Evangelical position, since it certainly seems to work. Preachers must ever remember that their task is not to be popular or successful, but to be faithful. The popular view among many (even fundamentalists) is the concept that if one is truly filled with the Spirit, one will build a large and successful work. While, in God's providence, some may do this, not all will. Scripture is replete with examples of people who faithfully followed their Lord but were not successful by human standards. John the Baptist for a while was very successful, and large numbers repented and were baptized under his preaching. But difficult days came upon him. His crowds began to dwindle, and his life was eventually taken by his enemies. But he received the high commendation of Christ who called him "my messenger" and declared that there had been no human prophet greater than John the Baptist (Matt. 11:10-11). As each servant of God is faithful to his Master, he will receive from his Master that which is his due. Some will be extraordinarily successful in man's eyes and will receive accolades, be invited to deliver lectures on "how-to-do-it," and be honored in ecclesiastical circles. Others, equally faithful, may suffer many defeats and hardships, may never have a work that is viewed as significant, and may labor for their entire ministry in the backwaters of Christendom. "A man can receive nothing, except it be given him from heaven" (John 3:27). We should never compromise God's truth in order to try to be something that God does not want us to be. We should labor for God's glory alone without thought to our self-aggrandizement.

The Perception That New Evangelicals Are More Loving

One young man who had been for years a member of a fundamentalist church suddenly left it to join a New Evangelical congregation. Upon enquiring as to the reason, the pastor was told that the New Evangelicals were more loving than the fundamentalists and that the young man was attracted to them for this reason. None of us can claim a corner on love, and no doubt it is true that many fundamentalist congregations could greatly improve in their love toward the Lord, toward one another, and toward the world in which they live. However, what some perceive of as love is, in reality, compromise. Many confuse a broad acceptance of various doctrinal positions, lifestyles, musical tastes, and methodologies as a demonstration of Christian love. In other words, if one is broader and more lenient, one is more loving. But this concept is not grounded in Scripture. Truth and love are not to be divorced. They walk together and are in perfect agreement. Some believe that if one is truly loving, one will not denounce error nor evaluate in a negative way the positions of others. Since New Evangelicals do not do this, they are perceived to be more loving than fundamentalists, to be kinder, more gracious, and more tolerant. But divine love is capable of hatred, strange as that may seem. "Ye that love the Lord, hate evil" (Ps. 97:10). We are to "love in the truth" (II John 1). One who is truly filled with divine love will rebuke evil and expose error. Many have erroneously equated a refusal to speak forthrightly as a demonstration of love.

Gradually Sliding into New Evangelicalism

David Beale warned against those who bear the label *fundamentalist* but whose personal philosophy is essentially New Evangelical. "Unlike present-day Fundamentalists, they refuse to regard the militant defense of the faith and the full doctrine and practice of holiness as intrinsically fundamental."[1] In other words, there are fundamentalists who are either becoming or already are New Evangelicals. Some are actually adopting New Evangelical philosophies while still proclaiming that they are not New Evangelicals. The basic problem is this: Many fundamentalists, when speaking of the New Evangelicalism, are referring to the original positions and writings of the early founders of New Evangelicalism such as Carl Henry and Harold Ockenga. They repudiate heartily the thoughts of these earlier leaders, but either in ignorance or willingly, they fail to recognize the updated version, the "new" New Evangelicalism. It is always safer to berate the teachings of those historically farther removed rather than of those who are currently afflicting the church.

In Educational Institutions

Christian colleges and theological seminaries have a tremendous impact upon the church as a whole. Local churches reflect the theological positions and attitudes that are found in schools of learning. Theological liberalism was spread like a virus throughout the professing church by unbelieving faculty members in schools supported by the giving of God's people. Likewise New Evangelicalism has been spread through the influence of schools where its proponents are teaching. In an enlightening article entitled "New Evangelical Churches Promoting Ecumenical Spirit," a reporter described the educational background of a local New Evangelical pastor: "A great deal of his learning came while working for his doctorate at an interdenominational seminary in Illinois. . . . There he learned respect for different strains of Christianity. 'It wasn't an overnight acceptance of people from a wide variety of traditions.' But slowly his 'bias' was whittled away."[2]

Unfortunately, what some perceive as the eradication of "bias" is really the erosion of biblical conviction. In warning against those who pretend to be what they are not, Schaeffer observed, "They should not hide in Christian institutions built by orthodox Christian conservatives with blood, sweat, and tears over years of work, using those same institutions to purvey views that would make the founders of such institutions roll over in their graves."[3] The founders of many a former fundamentalist school would be chagrined indeed to return and discover what is being taught in those institutions today.

Some fundamentalist institutions have been moved toward compromising positions through *financial pressures*. Fundamentalist colleges and seminaries historically have had to struggle financially. As the pressure mounts, the school administrators ponder how they may save the institution. They feel they must broaden their base of support. To do this will require a broadening of their position so as to attract those of other persuasions. Gradually this "broadening" occurs—all, of course, in the name of enlightenment and progress.

Ongoing *faculty education* can be an Achilles heel to a fundamentalist school. In order to improve their academic status, both colleges and seminaries encourage their faculty members to pursue advanced degrees. Most of the schools offering such degrees are New Evangelical in persuasion. While some faculty members are able to attend such institutions and still retain their separatist convictions, many are not. There are goodly numbers of professedly fundamentalist, separatist institutions whose positions are continually compromised by faculty members whose minds were contaminated with New Evangelical views while pursuing master's and doctor's programs.

Emphasis upon the possession of prestigious *academic credentials* has ruined many an institution. Having been the president of a Christian college for many years as well as the president of three seminaries, this writer is well aware of the need for academic credibility. However, far too many administrators in professedly fundamentalist institutions are more concerned with filling their faculty with Ph.D.'s than with finding people who have deep doctrinal and spiritual convictions. Many (not all) persons with high academic credentials lack commitment to fundamentalist separatism. They are mainly interested in a job and will be more than happy to adjust their convictions in a suitable fashion. To maintain strong fundamentalist schools requires dedicated faculty members, people of conviction who from their hearts believe in the position of the institution and do not hesitate to indoctrinate their students in the correct way of the Lord. New Evangelicals do not want to indoctrinate. They sneer at what they call the "Bible school mentality" that sets forth specific doctrinal positions to students as authoritative rather than tentative. Some administrators of erstwhile fundamentalist schools promote that sort of approach to education, thinking they are being "progressive" and teaching students to think rather than merely accept what the professor teaches. We have no quarrel with efforts to make students think. But developing the thought process is not incompatible with authoritative teaching.

Professedly fundamentalist schools can gradually be weakened because of *a lack of required, systematic instruction in the errors of the apostasy as well as the New Evangelicalism*. It is often assumed by academic leaders that young people coming to separatist institutions are knowledgeable concerning the history and biblical foundations of the separatist movement. They are not. Years ago someone observed, "You cannot perpetuate a position without adequately trained personnel." Youth in our separatist schools who are going to be future leaders in our local churches need to be exposed to the reasons that the separatist cause exists.

Most fundamentalist colleges and seminaries still have required chapel. In many chapels, however, there is a notable *absence of messages on ecclesiastical separation*. While, on the one hand, we ought not to offer a steady diet of such instruction, on the other hand we should not neglect the subject either. Leaders of the institution should bring messages from time to time in this vital area, and competent visiting speakers should be encouraged to do so as well. There are numerous institutions that would claim to be fundamentalist, separatist schools where these subjects are never discussed.

An institution is no stronger than its faculty. A separatist institution can harbor *faculty members who have hidden sympathies for the New Evangelicalism*. Thank God for the host of faculty members who serve sacrificially in fundamentalist, separatist institutions.

161

Many of these are fully supportive of the position of the institution. Not all may be, however. Some are job-seekers who will acquiesce outwardly to whatever is required to obtain employment but will chafe inwardly under the strict position on biblical separation. Such people can wield tremendous influence over students. It is not always what they say, but what they do not say. Many an institution has had its strong position gradually eroded by faculty members who are not committed to a biblical position.

A failure to distinguish between historic New Evangelicalism and current forms of New Evangelicalism weakens the testimony of many schools. If a pastor inquires as to the position of the institution with regard to New Evangelicalism, he will be told that it stands opposed. However, upon further discussion it will often be discovered that the institution is not really standing against contemporary New Evangelicalism. As we have already observed, the New Evangelicalism has proceeded far beyond its original form. Today's separatist schools must recognize the current expression of the New Evangelicalism, guard their borders against the intrusion of the same, and be willing to wage a militant warfare against it.

Speaking of militancy, it should be noted that many institutions have *a dread of being thought of as too negative or combative.* I remember the dean of a fundamentalist school who remarked to me on one occasion, "We are a separatist school, but we are not militant." But Rolland McCune is correct when he states, "Historic fundamentalism has always been characterized by militancy. . . . Militancy has to do with being aggressive and firm."[4] Marsden comments, "What chiefly distinguished fundamentalism from earlier evangelicalism was its militancy toward modernist theology and cultural change."[5] A biblical position cannot be maintained without militancy. When the apostle Paul drew near to the end of his earthly journey he wrote, "I have fought a good fight" (II Tim. 4:7). His entire life and ministry had been characterized by a battle. He was laying down his armor and entering into the presence of the commander in chief. To be militant does not mean to be nasty, vituperative, or mean-spirited. Failure to understand this truth causes some to disdain the term "militant." No one was more loving than the Apostle Paul, but no one was more bold and specific in his defense of the faith.

In Church Fellowships, Associations, or Denominations

While many local churches are completely unaffiliated with any group, others are a part of some metropolitan, regional, state, or national fellowship of churches. Some national fellowships are referred to as "denominations," though not all that are in such groups accept the term.

There are benefits to be derived from interchurch fellowships, but there are also potential dangers. When error begins to intrude into an organized group of churches, member churches can be more easily contaminated. Leaders of church organizations find it difficult to admit that there is anything amiss. To do so would be to reflect upon their leadership and suggest that they have been less than watchful. Leaders, therefore, will *emphatically deny that there has been any change.* "We stand just where we have always stood" will be the reassuring litany. While any objective observer can plainly see that the stance of the organization has changed, those intent on protecting the image of the group will steadfastly deny that fact. Unfortunately, leaders of some organizations that have been invaded by New Evangelical thought are so loyal to the body of which they are a part that they are blinded to the increasing deviations that are apparent to others. One is reminded of the Laodicean church that was totally oblivious to the spiritual loss it had suffered and strenuously proclaimed that they had "need of nothing" (Rev. 3:17).

New Evangelicalism can slip in the back door of church fellowships on the coattails of *pleas for a tolerance of diversity.* Often there is the call for more openness. Those calling for a more strict adherence to biblical standards are solemnly warned that to do so would be to violate "soul liberty" or "church autonomy." Some church fellowships that historically have stood strong for biblical separation have had their moorings undermined by just such arguments as these. Those who harbor New Evangelical concepts and practices (even though they may not call them such) are allowed to remain within the fellowship, and, even more serious, are placed in positions of leadership from which they can infect others.

When critics of an organization point out the inconsistencies of some brethren within the group, leaders of the group issue a warning against "wounding our own soldiers." This warning is often accompanied by a plea to *forget insignificant differences and unite in the task of world evangelism.* What some brethren, however, view as "insignificant differences" can be very critical differences indeed. The intrusion of alien and unbiblical philosophies and practices into the army of the Lord requires challenging some of the soldiers who have brought them in.

Strong loyalty to one's church fellowship can blind one to evident signs of developing weakness within that group. I remember many years ago when some of us were fighting against the incursions of the New Evangelicalism into the Conservative Baptist movement. At our annual convention in Detroit, Charles Woodbridge was asked to speak on the subject of the New Evangelicalism. He did a masterful job of delineating the sources, the progression, and the characteristics of the movement. As some of us were descending in an elevator after the session, a seminary president and one of the chief spokesmen for the New Evangelicalism within the Conservative Baptist movement was asked what he thought of Woodbridge's address. He replied, "He had a lot of interesting points, but none of them apply to our Conservative Baptist fellowship." The fact of the matter was, however, that at that very time the Conservative Baptists were riddled with New Evangelicalism.

Unwarranted assumptions often weaken groups. Because they were founded upon separatist principles, many groups assume that all of their present members understand and accept those principles. This is not always the case. Diligent and continuous instruction is required in order to inculcate truth into the minds of succeeding generations. God was very emphatic with the children of Israel that they should see that each generation was taught the Word of the Lord: "And thou shalt teach them diligently unto thy children, and shalt talk of them when thou sittest in thine house, and when thou walkest by the way, and when thou liest down, and when thou risest up" (Deut. 6:7). Surely this admonition applies to instruction in separatist principles as well as to all other truths of the Word of God. Some have the notion, however, that the battles for the faith are over and that we can now go on to other things.

The great prophet Elijah was an outspoken separatist. No fellowship would he have with the apostate Ahab and his scheming wife Jezebel. Thus, when Ahab met his adversary, he asked, "Art thou he that troubleth Israel?" (I Kings 18:17). What irony is here!

Here stood the man who led Israel into Baal worship, erected sites for the disgusting worship of that pagan deity, and "did more to provoke the Lord God of Israel to anger than all the kings of Israel that were before him" (I Kings 16:33). Yet he has the gall to call Elijah a troublemaker. People who are spiritual "prophets" within Christian organizations, speaking out against dangerous trends and compromises, are seldom popular with the leaders. They are viewed as "troublemakers," "insensitive," "uncooperative," and "hyper-fundamentalists." While it is true that some people are overly scrupulous and become "minutiae detectives," this fact should not be used to deny the properly expressed concerns of those who have legitimate evidence of deviation in important matters. It is true that "evil communications [company] corrupt good manners [character]" (I Cor. 15:33). Martyn Lloyd-Jones warned, "Be careful with whom you associate if you want to stand fast in the faith. You have got to avoid false teaching, to avoid error, to avoid wrong practice."[6] Another writer has made an interesting observation: "For an orthodoxy to remain hermetic it must be highly 'pollution conscious' and be capable of rejecting that pollution when the moral order is breached."[7] Many organizations find it impossible to maintain their purity. They cannot "reject pollution."

In Mission Boards

Thousands of missionaries have been sent around the world through the agency of Bible-believing mission boards. Many of the faith mission boards arose out of the fundamentalist-modernist conflict as fundamentalists repudiated the liberal influence within many denominations and founded boards independent of denominational control in order to be channels for sending sound missionaries to the fields of the world. However, mission boards are subject to the siren call of New Evangelicalism. Some boards that once took a strong stand for the fundamentalist position have yielded to the pressures of the times and either embraced or become tolerant of the New Evangelicalism.

The ever-present *financial pressures* have caused some to search for a broader base of support and thus water down their position so as to attract more individuals and churches. Leaders should always beware the subtle temptation to compromise a position in order to fill one's coffers. "For your heavenly Father

165

knoweth that ye have need of these things" (Matt. 6:32). Furthermore, in that same passage Christ connects the doing of "righteousness" with the provision of "these things" (material needs; Matt. 6:33). Our first obligation is not to seek to provide our material needs but to honor God and do what is right. "But my God shall supply all your need according to his riches in glory by Christ Jesus" (Phil. 4:19). God takes care of us as we obey His Word.

The recruitment of students from nonseparatist schools can weaken the fabric of a mission board. While it is true that students can sometimes be committed separatists despite the weak position of the institution they attended, such will be the exception and not the rule. Mission boards must be very careful about whom they appoint. A four-year stint in an institution whose leadership and faculty are not strongly fundamentalist will leave its impact upon even the finest and most dedicated students. The adverse effects of such an education will not be eradicated by a few hours of lectures in an orientation seminar or by the required reading of a few books. Because potential missionary candidates may like the general set-up of a mission board and agree with its doctrinal statement, they will acquiesce to its stated position on separation without really understanding it with all its implications. When they take up their ministry in another country and face critical issues, they do not know how to stand.

Objectionable and unwise alignments with compromising groups can injure the separatist witness of a mission board. These alignments may be either at home or on the mission field. In order to provide some service or meet some need, mission leaders sometimes form cooperative bonds with certain organizations that may not take their position but whose help is convenient. This can bring the mission into question with supporting pastors and churches. It can also create vexing problems for missionaries on the field whose convictions will not allow them to reach as far as their mission desires them to reach for fellowship. Should they compromise their convictions for the sake of unity within their mission, or should they speak up, seek to correct the situation, and thus risk alienation from their fellow missionaries as well as mission leaders and possibly eventual withdrawal from the mission? These are very real problems for many missionaries. Because their mission board has adopted a spirit of compromise, some godly servants of Christ have had to make painful decisions and leave that board with which they have served for many years. While some would like to think that struggles over the New Evangelicalism are "Western" in origin and thus have little relevance within the worldwide missionary enterprise, such is far from the case. Deviations from the doctrines and practices of God's Word most certainly have an impact upon the work of carrying out the Great Commission.

The election or appointment of weak board members can jeopardize the position of a mission agency. There are many "nice" men who have a concern for missions and are willing to serve on a mission board. They may not, however, be very militant and vigilant in their position on ecclesiastical separation. Before enlisting a board member, one needs to know about his track record. Has he been a consistent and outspoken separatist? Does he evidence deep convictions? Many pastors and laymen are added to boards because they lead large and prosperous churches, or because they are influential or wealthy. Sometimes little attention is given to their convictions on separation.

In Local Churches

Scripture is clear that the local church is "the pillar and ground of the truth" (I Tim. 3:15). God's work in this dispensation of grace is to be carried on through the instrumentality of the local church. It is natural, therefore, that the Devil would seek by every means possible to corrupt and weaken the local church.

Uninformed or indifferent pastors certainly aid in the spread of New Evangelical principles among local congregations. Many pastors were never exposed to teaching on the subject in college or seminary and are ignorant, therefore, of the nature and dangers of New Evangelicalism. Even some who have been exposed to such teaching have turned away from it to embrace New Evangelical thought. Obviously a local church will reflect the teaching of its pastor. Many churches that once were strong fundamentalist centers have gradually degenerated in their position through weak leadership.

Many pastors find themselves under considerable *pressure from members of their church*. Some of these members have perhaps moved into the church from other churches that were of New Evangelical persuasion. Others have been influenced by the writings of current New Evangelicals. Still others have friends who have New Evangelical leanings. Many are also influenced by local Christian radio stations that feature an abundance of New Evangelical teaching and music. The separatist pastor often feels himself besieged by alien forces as he tries to lead his people in the right direction. Many pastors have felt obligated to resign because they felt they did not have the church leadership with them as they struggled against the New Evangelical philosophy.

As we have already mentioned, *the affiliations of a local church* can be either a blessing or a curse. Some churches find themselves in church associations where perhaps they have been for years. These associations, however, are deteriorating in their fundamentalist stance, and the churches that comprise them are being adversely affected by it. It is usually quite difficult to persuade a congregation to vote out of an associational group to which it has belonged for a long time. The pastor may jeopardize his own position in the church by even suggesting such a thing. However, if there are New Evangelical tendencies within that group, local churches will be tainted with them through interchurch conferences, denominational magazines or other literature which they use, and the ministry of leaders within the group who may visit their church.

We have noted earlier that *obsession with growth, bigness, and success* characterize New Evangelicalism. One of the early founders of New Evangelicalism has himself pointed out the problem:

> Many evangelicals now measure growth mainly in terms of numbers; distinctions of doctrine and practice are subordinated in a broad welcome for charismatic, Catholic, traditional and other varieties of evangelicals. Theological differences are minimized by evangelical publishers and publications reaching for mass circulation, by evangelicals luring capacity audiences and even by evangelism festivals seeking the largest possible involvement. Church growth seminars have even embraced "miracle-growth" churches that claim to raise the dead and to reproduce all other apostolic gifts. Numerical bigness has become an infectious epidemic.[8]

Fundamentalist pastors, goaded by their desire to see numerical growth, visit "growth seminars," almost always manned by New Evangelicals. In the process of supposedly learning how to "grow" their church, they also imbibe the philosophies of New Evangelicalism. They see no problem, however, because "it works."

Perhaps nothing precipitates a slide toward New Evangelicalism more than the *introduction of Contemporary Christian Music.* Pastors of large churches inform us that we cannot hope to attract the masses with the old, outdated church music. We must change our style so as to catch the attention of the godless. "Services are often created to minimize discomfort for the unbeliever so that he or she begins to accept Christianity as an affirming influence. People ought to leave church feeling good about themselves, it is said, instead of being called to self-examination, sincere repentance, and faith toward God."[9]

One of the chief ways of making a church more "contemporary" is to introduce contemporary music, of which there is a great abundance available. This inevitably leads toward a gradual slide in other areas as well until the entire church is infiltrated by ideas and programs alien to the original position of the church.

The current *fascination with so-called Christian psychology* has led many a congregation down the primrose path to compromise. Speakers with this kind of emphasis abound. Books espousing this viewpoint are prolific. One can obtain videos by the hundreds that present various aspects of psychology that purportedly are based upon Christian principles. An undue preoccupation with this subject has carried many of God's people away from the solid truths of Scripture and into the land of human fancies created by an overdependence upon secular psychological theories. The quotation of a few Scripture verses does not sanctify the psychological concepts coming from the minds of unsaved men. Emphasis upon psychology has helped to feed the prevalent notion that Scripture is only important if it meets our "felt needs." It contributes to a self-centered instead of a God-centered theology and ministry.

One emphasis found more and more in churches today is popular but dangerous. It is the tendency to view the local church primarily as *a haven of fellowship rather than a center of theological teaching.* Certainly Christian fellowship has its proper place. It should not, however, be the "be-all and end-all" of the church's existence. Many moderns are looking for "support" rather than salvation, assistance in their daily problems rather than the development of a holy life, and a circle of spiritual equals rather than an authoritative spiritual teacher. A strong emphasis has arisen on the development of small groups within the church to provide

169

meaningful fellowship for hurting saints. This is not in and of itself a bad thing, but it does have ominous overtones.

> What many are looking for is a spiritual social club, an institution that offers convivial relationships but avoids influencing people on how they live or what they believe. Whenever the church does assert a historically orthodox position, one that might in some way restrict an individual's doing whatever he or she chooses, the church is accused of being "out of touch"—as if its beliefs are to be determined by majority vote or market surveys. Spiritual consumers are interested not in what the church stands for but in the fulfillment it can deliver.[10]

Historically, fundamentalist churches have taken a definite stand against worldliness. However, today, in the face of charges that to do so is "legalistic," more and more churches are opting for general statements, if they have any at all. Gone are the leadership standards which prohibit drinking or smoking on the part of church leaders. They have been replaced with nonspecific statements such as, "We should do all things to glorify God." If Sunday school teachers feel they can take a drink of liquor occasionally "to the glory of God," they may exercise their Christian liberty to do so. Pastors, fearful of being castigated as "legalists," have succumbed to the popular demand for less stringent standards.

A general *spirit of accommodation evidenced in an evangelical ecumenism* is very prevalent today. A newspaper article entitled, "New Evangelical Churches Promoting Ecumenical Spirit" nicely summarizes this trend:

> Now a new ecumenical spirit, the same force that has drawn mainline denominations into cooperative efforts, is sweeping through many of the more evangelical and conservative congregations nationally. . . . The result of the ecumenism is mutual acceptance and support, and that is attracting more members, leaders say. It is also blurring denominational lines, drawing many of those churches a bit closer to mainline denominations, and also making it easier for Christians to move from one conservative church to another, and from mainline churches to evangelical ones.[11]

The above-described tendencies are evident in many churches that formerly were unashamedly fundamentalist and separatistic local churches. Many of them would strongly deny that they are sympathetic to the New Evangelicalism. The "gray hairs" that mark deterioration of strength and loss of vitality have appeared, "yet he knoweth it not" (Hos. 7:9). Unconscious spiritual loss—it is the worst kind. To have slipped from a strong biblical position and not be aware of it is a tragedy of the most profound dimensions. To have retreated, but not be conscious of your retreat, is most embarrassing.

Conclusion

What should the pastor, missionary, and church member do who wishes to honor God and who sees the deadly dangers of the New Evangelicalism? He should take the "whole armour of God" and "stand" (Eph. 6:13). This implies that there is a position to be defended, a divinely revealed position from which we should not be driven. It involves a conflict, an unending battle. It will involve controversy with other believers who are failing to stand. This controversy should be conducted with Christian grace and under the control of the Holy Spirit, but such controversy cannot be escaped. The New Evangelicalism is robbing Christ's church of theological accuracy and is corrupting its holy character. Fundamentalists must contest its inroads and challenge its precepts. May it please God to raise up a great host of His people who will do battle for His glory.

Notes

[1]David Beale, *In Pursuit of Purity,* pp. 261ff.

[2]"New Evangelical Churches Promoting Ecumenical Spirit," *Minneapolis Star-Tribune,* 28 May 1989.

[3]Franky Schaeffer, *Bad News For Modern Man,* p. 80.

[4]Rolland McCune, "Fundamentalism in the 1980's and 1990's," Unpublished paper, 1990.

[5]George Marsden, *Understanding Fundamentalism and Evangelicalism,* p. 66.

[6]Ian Murray, *David Martyn Lloyd-Jones: The Fight of Faith,* p. 608.

[7]Mary Douglas, *Purity and Danger,* p. 161.

[8]Carl Henry, *Confessions of a Theologian,* p. 387.

[9]Don Matzat, "A Better Way: Christ Is My Worth," *Power Religion,* edited by Michael Scott Horton, p. 253.

[10]Charles Colson, "Welcome to McChurch," *Christianity Today,* 23 November 1992, p. 30.

[11]"New Evangelical Churches Promoting Ecumenical Spirit," *Minneapolis Star-Tribune.*

Selected Bibliography

Books

Anderson, Leith. *A Church for the 21st Century.* Minneapolis: Bethany House Publishers, 1992.

————. *Dying for Change.* Minneapolis: Bethany House Publishers, 1990.

Ashbrook, John. *New Neutralism II.* Mentor, Ohio: Here I Stand Books, 1992.

Barna, George. *The Frog in the Kettle.* Ventura, Calif.: Regal Books, 1990.

————. *Marketing the Church.* Colorado Springs: NavPress, 1988.

————. *User Friendly Churches.* Ventura, Calif.: Regal Books, 1991.

Barr, James. *Beyond Fundamentalism.* Philadelphia: Westminster Press, 1984.

————. *Fundamentalism.* Philadelphia: Westminster Press, 1977.

Beale, David O. *In Pursuit of Purity.* Greenville, S.C.: Unusual Publications, 1986.

Beegle, Dewey. *The Inspiration of Scripture.* Philadelphia: Westminster Press, 1963.

Bloesch, Donald. *Crumbling Foundations: Death and Rebirth in an Age of Upheaval.* Grand Rapids: Zondervan, 1984.

————. *The Evangelical Renaissance.* Grand Rapids: Eerdmans, 1973.

————. *The Future of Evangelical Christianity.* Colorado Springs: Helmers and Howard, 1988.

Bobgan, Martin and Deidre. *Prophets of Psychoheresy I.* Santa Barbara, Calif.: EastGate Publishers, 1989.

————. *Prophets of Psychoheresy II.* Santa Barbara, Calif.: EastGate Publishers, 1990.

————. *Psychoheresy.* Santa Barbara, Calif.: EastGate Publishers, 1987.

Budgen, Victor. *The Charismatics and the Word of God.* Welwyn, England: Evangelical Press, 1985.

Dobson, Edward. *In Search of Unity.* New York: Thomas Nelson, 1985.

Douglas, Mary. *Purity and Danger.* London: Routledge and Kegan Paul, 1966.

Durant, Will. *The Story of Philosophy.* New York: Washington Square Press, 1961.

Edgar, Thomas R. *Miraculous Gifts: Are They for Today?* Neptune, N.J.: Loiseaux Brothers, 1983.

Ellingsen, Mark. *The Evangelical Movement.* Minneapolis: Augsburg Publishing House, 1988.

Erickson, Millard. *The New Evangelical Theology.* Westwood, N.J.: Fleming H. Revell Company, 1968.

Fant, David J. *A. J. Tozer: A Twentieth Century Prophet.* Harrisburg, Pa.: Christian Publications, 1964.

Gromacki, Robert. *The Modern Tongues Movement.* Philadelphia: Presbyterian and Reformed, 1967.

Guiness, Os. *The Gravedigger File.* Downers Grove, Ill.: Inter-Varsity Press, 1983.

Hatfield, Mark. *Conflict and Conscience.* Waco: Word Books, 1971.

Heldenbrand, Richard L. *Christianity and New Evangelical Philosophies.* Winona Lake, Ind.: Richard Heldenbrand, 1989.

Henry, Carl. *Confessions of A Theologian.* Waco: Word Books, 1986.

Horton, Michael Scott. *Made in America: The Shaping of Modern American Evangelicalism.* Grand Rapids: Baker Book House, 1991.

Horton, Michael Scott, ed. *Power Religion.* Chicago: Moody Press, 1992.

Hubbard, David. *What We Believe and Teach.* Pasadena: Fuller Theological Seminary, n.d.

Hunt, Dan, and McMahon, T. A. *The Seduction of Christianity.* Eugene, Ore.: Harvest House Publishers, 1985.

Hunter, James Davison. *American Evangelicalism: Conservative Religion and the Quandary of Modernity.* New Brunswick, N.J.: Rutgers University Press, 1983.

———. *Evangelicalism: The Coming Generation.* Chicago: University of Chicago Press, 1987.

Johnston, Jon. *Will Evangelicalism Survive Its Own Popularity?* Grand Rapids: Zondervan, 1980.

Johnston, Robert K. *Evangelicals at an Impasse.* Atlanta: John Knox Press, 1978.

Jones, Bob. *Cornbread and Caviar: Reminiscence and Reflections.* Greenville, S.C.: Bob Jones University Press, 1985.

Kantzer, Kenneth, ed. *Evangelical Roots.* New York: Thomas Nelson Publishers, 1978.

Kennedy, Gerald. *God's Good News.* New York: Harper, 1955.

Lasch, Christopher. *The Culture of Narcissism.* New York: Warner, 1979.

Larson, Bruce. *The Relational Revolution.* Waco: Word Books, 1976.

Lewis, Gregory. *Is God for Sale?* Wheaton, Ill.: Tyndale, 1979.

Lightner, Robert P. *Neoevangelicalism Today.* Schaumburg, Ill.: Regular Baptist Press, 1978.

Lindsell, Harold. *The Battle for the Bible.* Grand Rapids: Zondervan, 1976.

———. *The Bible in the Balance.* Grand Rapids: Zondervan, 1979.

MacArthur, John. *Charismatic Chaos.* Grand Rapids: Zondervan, 1992.

———. *Our Sufficiency in Christ.* Dallas: Word Books, 1991.

McGavran, Donald. *Understanding Church Growth.* Grand Rapids: Eerdmans, 1970.

Machen, J. Gresham. *Christianity and Liberalism.* 1923. Reprint. Grand Rapids: Eerdmans, 1974.

Marsden, George, ed. *Evangelicalism and Modern America.* Grand Rapids: Eerdmans, 1984.

————. *Fundamentalism and American Culture.* New York: Oxford University Press, 1980.

————. *Reforming Fundamentalism.* Grand Rapids: Eerdmans, 1987.

————. *Understanding Fundamentalism and Evangelicalism.* Grand Rapids: Eerdmans, 1991.

Mayers, Marvin K.; Richards, Lawrence O.; and Webber, Robert. *Reshaping Evangelical Higher Education,* edited by . Grand Rapids: Zondervan, 1972.

Miller, Donald. *The Case for Liberal Christianity.* San Francisco: Harper and Row, 1981.

Morris, Henry. *Studies in the Bible and Science.* Philadelphia: Presbyterian and Reformed, 1966.

Murch, James Deforest. *Cooperation Without Compromise: A History of the National Association of Evangelicals.* Grand Rapids: Eerdmans, 1956.

Murray, Ian H. *David Martyn Lloyd-Jones: The Fight of Faith.* Edinburgh: The Banner of Truth Trust, 1990.

Myers, Kenneth. *All God's Children and Blue Suede Shoes.* Westchester, Ill.: Crossway Books, 1989.

Nash, Ronald. *The New Evangelicalism.* Grand Rapids: Zondervan, 1963.

Neve, J. L. *A History of Christian Thought.* Philadelphia: Muhlenberg Press, 1946.

Nida, Eugene. *Message and Mission.* New York: Harper and Brothers, 1960.

————, and Taber, Charles. *The Theory and Practice of Translation.* Leiden, Netherlands: United Bible Societies, Briss, 1969.

Noll, Mark, and Wells, David eds. *Christian Faith and Practice in the Modern World.* Grand Rapids: Eerdmans, 1988.

Oden, Thomas. *Agenda for Theology.* San Francisco: Harper and Row, 1979.

Pattison, Robert. *The Triumph of Vulgarity: Rock Music in the Mirror of Romanticism.* New York: Oxford University Press, 1987.

Penner, James. *Goliath: The Life of Robert Schuller.* Anaheim: New Hope Publication Cathedral Press, 1992.

Pickering, Ernest. *Biblical Separation.* Schaumburg, Ill.: Regular Baptist Press, 1979.

————. *Charismatic Confusion.* Schaumburg, Ill.: Regular Baptist Press, n.d.

Quebedeaux, Richard. *The New Charismatics.* New York: Doubleday and Company, 1976.

————. *The Worldly Evangelicals.* San Francisco: Harper and Row Publishers, 1978.

————. *The Young Evangelicals.* New York: Harper and Row, 1974.

Ramm, Bernard. *After Fundamentalism.* San Francisco: Harper and Row, 1983.

————. *The Evangelical Heritage.* Waco: Word Books, 1973.

Reich, Charles. *The Greening of America.* New York: Random House, 1970.

Rogers, Jack. *Confessions of a Conservative Evangelical.* Philadelphia: Westminster Press, 1974.

————, and McKim, Donald. *The Authority and Interpretation of the Bible.* New York: Harper and Row, 1979.

Schaeffer, Francis. *The Church Before the Watching World.* Downer's Grove, Ill.: Inter-Varsity Press, 1971.

————. *The Great Evangelical Disaster.* Westchester, Ill.: Crossway Books, 1984.

Schaeffer, Franky. *Bad News for Modern Man.* Westchester, Ill.: Crossway Books, 1984.

Schuller, Robert. *Self-Esteem: The New Reformation.* Waco: Word Books, 1982.

Shelley, Bruce. *Evangelicalism in America.* Grand Rapids: Eerdmans, 1967.

Smedes, Lewis. *Sex for Christians.* Grand Rapids: Eerdmans, 1976.

Sweet, Leonard, ed. *The Evangelical Tradition in America.* Macon, Ga.: Mercer University Press, 1984.

Swindoll, Charles. *The Grace Awakening.* Dallas: Word Books, 1990.

Webber, Robert, and Bloesch, Donald. *The Orthodox Evangelicals.* New York: Thomas Nelson Publishers, 1978.

Wells, David, and Woodbridge, John D. *The Evangelicals.* New York: Abingdon Press, 1975.

Williamson, Peter, and Perrotta, Kevin. *Christianity Confronts Modernity.* Ann Arbor: Servant Books, 1981.

Woodbridge, John; Noll, Mark; and Hatch, Nathan. *The Gospel in America.* Grand Rapids: Zondervan, 1979.

Wuthnow, Robert. *The Struggle for America's Soul.* Grand Rapids: Eerdmans, 1989.

Book Articles

Campbell, Donald. "Galatians." In *The Bible Knowledge Commentary,* vol. 2. Wheaton, Ill.: Victor Books, 1983.

Carpenter, Joel. "The Fundamentalist Leaven and the Rise of an Evangelical United Front." In *The Evangelical Tradition in America,* edited by Leonard Sweet. Macon, Ga.: Mercer University Press, 1984.

Clark, Stephen. "Modern Approaches to Scriptural Authority." In *Christianity Confronts Modernity,* edited by Peter Williamson and Kevin Perrota. Ann Arbor: Servant Books, 1981.

Fraser, Eloise Renich. "Evangelical Feminism: The Threat of its Survival." In *Evangelicalism: Surviving its Success,* edited by David Fraser. Princeton: Princeton University Press, 1987.

LaSor, William. "Life Under Tension." In *The Authority of Scripture at Fuller.* Pasadena: Fuller Theological Seminary, n.d.

Lewis, C. S. "De Descriptione Temperum." In *They Asked for a Paper: Papers and Addresses.* London: Geoffrey Bles, 1962.

Marsden, George. "From Fundamentalism to Evangelicalism." In *The Evangelicals,* edited by David Wells and John Woodbridge. New York: Abingdon Press, 1975.

Ockenga, Harold. "From Fundamentalism Through New Evangelicalism to Evangelicalism." In *Evangelical Roots,* edited by Kenneth Kantzer. New York: Thomas Nelson Publishers, 1978.

Pinnock, Clark. "From Augustine to Arminius: A Pilgrimage in Theology." In *The Grace of God, the Will of Man,* edited by Clark Pinnock. Grand Rapids: Zondervan, 1989.

Reichley, A. James. "The Evangelical and Fundamentalist Revolt." In *Piety and Politics,* edited by Richard John Neuhaus and Michael Cromartie. Washington, D.C.: Ethics and Public Policy Center, 1987.

Savage, Peter. "The Church and Evangelism." In *The New Face of Evangelicalism,* edited by C. René Padilla. Downers Grove: Inter-Varsity Press, 1976.

Stott, John R. W. "Biblical Preaching Is Expository Preaching." In *Evangelical Roots,* edited by Kenneth Kantzer. New York: Thomas Nelson Publishers, 1978.

―――. Foreword to *Down To Earth,* edited by John R. W. Stott and Robert Coote. Grand Rapids: Eerdmans, 1980.

Wells, David. "An American Theology: The Painful Transition from Theoria to Praxis." In *Evangelicalism and Modern America,* edited by George Marsden. Grand Rapids: Eerdmans, 1984.

Wright, George Frederick. "The Passing of Evolution." In *The Fundamentals For Today,* edited by Charles Feinberg, vol. 2. Grand Rapids: Kregel Publications, 1958.

Periodical Articles

"A Conversation With the Young Evangelicals," *Post-American,* January 1975.

Ayer, William Ward. Letter to the Editor. *United Evangelical Action,* 15 June 1958.

"Billy Graham." *Time,* 20 March 1950.

"Billy Graham at NCC Assembly." *Christian Beacon,* 5 January 1967.

"Billy Graham's Crusade." *Sword of the Lord,* 10 April 1959.

Bockelman, Wilfred. "A Lutheran Looks at Billy Graham." *Lutheran Standard,* 10 October 1961.

Bron, Robert. "Evangelical Megashift." *Christianity Today,* 19 February 1990.

Colson, Charles. "Welcome to McChurch." *Christianity Today,* 23 November 1992.

Dunn, Charles. "Campus Crusade: Its Message and Methods." *Faith for the Family,* October 1980.

Evans, M. Stanton. "The Brainwashing of Billy Graham." *Human Events,* 5 June 1982.

Graham, Billy. Interview, "My Role Is to Bring Peace and Understanding." *USA Today,* 15 May 1985.

———. "Taking the World's Temperature: An Interview with Billy Graham." *Christianity Today,* 23 September 1977.

Gray, Robert. Interview, *Voice,* January 1977.

Hearn, Arnold. "Fundamentalist Renaissance." *Christian Century,* 30 April 1958.

Henry, Carl. "Conflict Over Biblical Inerrancy." *Christianity Today,* 7 May 1976.

———. "Firm on the Fundamentals." *Christianity Today,* 18 November 1988.

———. "The New Coalitions." *Christianity Today,* 17 September 1989.

———. "The Vigor of the New Evangelicalism." *Christian Life,* January 1948.

———. "YFC's 'Cheer For Jesus' No Substitute For The Apostles's Creed." *World,* 11 March 1990.

Howard, Tom, contributor. "On Not Leaving It to the Liberals." *Eternity,* February 1977.

Hull, Merle. "The U.S. Congress on Evangelism." *The Baptist Bulletin,* November 1969.

"Inside Washington." *Human Events,* 22 May 1982.

"Is Evangelical Theology Changing?" *Christian Life,* March 1956.

Jewett, Paul King. "Why I Favor the Ordination of Women." *Christianity Today,* 6 June 1975.

Kenneth Kantzer. Interview, "Reflections: Five Years of Change." *Christianity Today,* 26 November 1982.

Lindsell, Harold. "What or Who Is an Evangelical?" *Fundamentalist Journal,* February 1984.

Marty, Martin. "Reflections on Graham by a Former Grump." *Christianity Today,* 18 November 1988.

McCoy, John. "Evangelical Churches Have Foot in Each Camp." *Seattle Post-Intelligence,* 22 February 1986.

McIntosh, Gary L. "What's in a Name?" *The McIntosh Church Growth Network,* vol. 3, no. 5 (May 1991).

"Mighty Fortresses: Megachurches Strive to Be All Things To All Parishioners." *Wall Street Journal,* 13 May 1991.

Millheim, John. "A Consortium of Compromise." *Baptist Bulletin,* October 1974.

Neff, David. "The Down Side of Civility." *Christianity Today*, 6 February 1987.

"New Evangelical Churches Promoting Ecumenical Spirit." *Minneapolis Star-Tribune*, 28 May 1989.

"New Liberal Mood Is Found Among Fundamentalist Protestants." *The New York Times*, 14 September 1969.

Ockenga, Harold. "Resurgent Evangelical Leadership." *Christianity Today*, 10 October 1960.

"On Meeting Changing Issues," *Christianity Today*, 4 March 1957.

"Passing It On: Will Our Kids Recognize Our Faith?" *World*, 11 March 1989.

Perez, Jaffet. "Testimony." *Baptist Examiner*, 16 May 1964.

Peterson, J. Randall. "Evangelicalism: A Movement's Direction." *Evangelical Newsletter*, 20 December 1985.

Peterson, William. "The Mission in England." *Evangelical Newsletter*, 10 August 1984.

———. "The Present Status of the New Evangelicalism." *Minneapolis: Central Press*, n.d.

———. "Shortened Cords, Weakened Stakes: Peril of the New Evangelicalism." *The Gospel Witness*, 4 August 1966.

———. "What Is the New Evangelicalism?" *The Baptist Bulletin*, July 1960.

Pierhard, Richard. "Lausanne II: Reshaping World Evangelicalism." *Christian Century*, 16 August 1989.

Pinnock, Clark. "Making Theology Relevant." *Christianity Today*, 29 May 1981.

———. "The Arminian Option." *Christianity Today*, 19 February 1990.

———. "The Inerrancy Debate Among the Evangelicals." *Theology, News and Notes*, 1976.

Plowman, Edward. "Graham Joins Russian Church Festivities." *Christianity Today*, 15 July 1988.

Quebedeaux, Richard. "The Evangelicals: New Trends and New Tensions." *Christianity and Crisis*, 20 September 1976.

Ramm, Bernard. "Welcome 'Green-Grass' Evangelicals." *Eternity*, March 1974.

Reed, Doug. "Billy Graham: Maturing Leader." *Asheville Citizen Times*, 19 October 1958.

"Reuniting the Flock." *U.S. News and World Report*, 25 March 1991.

Reynolds, M. H. "Mikhail Gorbachev and Billy Graham." *Foundation*, September 1988.

Roddy, Sherman. "Fundamentalists and Ecumenicity." *Christian Century*, 1 October 1958.

Schaeffer, Francis A. Interview, "Schaeffer Reflects on 50 Years of Denominational Ins and Outs." *Christianity Today*, 10 April 1981.

Sheerin, John. "Dialogue With Evangelicals Like Billy Graham." *The Catholic World*, June 1965.

Shuler, Robert, editor. *The Methodist Challenge,* October 1957. Published by the Trinity Methodist Church, Los Angeles, Calif.

Taylor, G. Aiken. "Is God As Good As His Word?" *Christianity Today,* 4 February 1977.

"Theology, Evangelism, Ecumenism," editorial. *Christianity Today,* 20 January 1958.

Walt Malcolm. "Mission England: Is It Scriptural?" *Bible League Quarterly,* No. 336, January-March 1984.

Walvoord, John F. "The Lausanne Congress on Evangelism." *Voice,* March-April 1975.

Wells, Ronald. "Where My Generation Parts Company." *Eternity,* May 1970.

Weniger, G. Archer. "Graham At Oakland." *Sword of the Lord,* 19 November 1971.

White, W. R. "Modern Pharisees and Sadducees." *Baptist Standard,* 7 July 1958.

Wright, J. Elwin. "The Issue of Separation." *United Evangelical Action,* 14 August 1945.

Other Sources

Allen, Cuthbert E. Letter to Julius Taylor.

"The Chicago Call: An Appeal To Evangelicals." Westchester, Ill.: Cornerstone Press, 1977.

Graham, Billy. "Separation or Fellowship?" [an open letter].

Grounds, Vernon. "Fundamentalism and Evangelicalism: Legitimate Labels or Illicit Libels?" Denver: Conservative Baptist Theological Seminary (privately produced), n.d.

Ketcham, Robert T. "Special Information Bulletin #15," November 1962, General Association of Regular Baptist Churches.

McCune, Rolland. "Fundamentalism in the 1980's and 1990's." Detroit: Detroit Baptist Theological Seminary (unpublished paper), 1990.

Nissiotis, Nikos. Circular letter of October 1970. World Council of Churches Ecumenical Institute.

Reynolds, M. H. "Key '73: An Appraisal" (privately produced), n.d.

———. A report, "The Muddy Waters of Mainstream Evangelical Thought." October 1969.

Tassell, Paul. *Is Campus Crusade Scriptural?* Pamphlet published by Regular Baptist Press, n.d.

This We Believe. Milwaukee: Northwestern Publishing House, n.d.

Index

Fuller Theological Seminary 8,
11, 24-25, 27, 30, 32-33, 36, 41,
44, 78-79, 97, 100-101, 112, 128
Fundamentalism 4-6, 7-8, 17-18,
51-55, 63-64, 78, 80, 84, 97, 98,
156-71
Fundamentals, The 4, 81

Gallagher, Sharon 83
General Association of Regular
Baptist Churches 5
George Fox College 30
Gordon, A. J. 31
Gordon-Conwell Theological
Seminary 30, 98
Graham, Billy 11, 12, 34, 35, 38-
39, 40, 43, 49-74, 83, 87, 129
Grounds, Vernon 12, 20, 35

Hardesty, Nancy 77, 83
Hegel, George 2
Hell, doctrine of 103
Henry, Carl 10, 12, 14-15, 18, 34,
35, 38-39, 40, 78, 79, 93, 96-97,
99, 105, 111, 115, 159
Houghton College 30-31
Howard, Tom 84

Independent Fundamental
Churches of America 5, 41-42
Inspiration of Scripture 19-20, 31,
41, 78-79, 99-101, 147-48
International Conference for Itiner-
ant Evangelists 60
International Congress on World
Evangelization I (Lausanne) 39-42
International Congress on World
Evangelization II (Manila) 43

Jewett, Paul King 78, 83, 99, 109
Jones, Bob, Jr. 51
Jones, Bob, Sr. viii, 32, 49, 51

Kantzer, Kenneth 12, 77-78, 99
Kennedy, Gerald 56
Key '73 39, 89

Lausanne Covenant 41-42
Lausanne I; *see* International Con-
gress on World Evangelization I
"Legalism" 85, 86-87, 146, 170
Liberalism 3-4, 63-64, 67-68, 90
Lindsell, Harold 33, 34, 40, 78,
79, 97, 99
Lloyd-Jones, D. Martyn 26, 113,
140, 165
Local churches 131, 134-35, 145-
46, 167-70

McCarrell, William 5
Machen, J. Gresham 5, 20, 25-26,
31
McIntire, Carl 11, 38
Manila Manifesto 43
Methodist Challenge 5, 51
Methodist Federation for Social
Action 55
Militancy 11, 33, 162
Mission England 59
Missions and mission boards 103,
165-67
Modernism 1-2; *see also* Liberal-
ism
Moody Bible Institute 49
Moody, Dwight L. 49